I.T. ANSWERS
TO
H.R. QUESTIONS

Peter Kingsbury is currently a senior lecturer at the University of Luton, teaching in the human resource management and development department. He is a Fellow of the Institute of Personnel and Development. Prior to joining the University he worked as a self-employed management consultant for a number of years. Previously he had been a personnel director of a computer training company and was training and development manager with Eden Vale, which was part of Grand Metropolitan at the time. He has a degree in psychology, which he undertook through the Open University, and has completed a master's degree in software engineering management. He also holds a Certificate in Post-Compulsory Education. He is currently researching into the utilisation of the functionality of commercially available software.

developing practice

Other titles in the series:

Appraisal 2nd edition
Clive Fletcher

Benchmarking for People Managers
John Bramham

Counselling in the Workplace
Jenny Summerfield and Lyn van Oudtshoorn

Employee Attitude and Opinion Surveys
Mike Walters

From Absence to Attendance
Alastair Evans and Steve Palmer

The Job Evaluation Handbook
Michael Armstrong and Angela Baron

The Performance Management Handbook
Edited by Mike Walters

Project Management
Roland and Frances Bee

Recruitment and Selection
Gareth Roberts

Re-engineering's Missing Ingredient
Mike Oram and Richard S Wellins

360-degree Feedback
Peter Ward

The Institute of Personnel and Development is the leading pub-
lisher of books and reports for personnel and training professionals
and students and for all those concerned with the effective
management and development of people at work. For full details
of all our titles please telephone the Publishing Department on
0181 263 3387.

I.T. ANSWERS
TO
H.R. QUESTIONS

Peter Kingsbury

INSTITUTE OF PERSONNEL AND DEVELOPMENT

© Peter Kingsbury 1997

First published in 1997

All rights reserved. No part of this publication may be
reproduced, stored in a retrieval system, or transmitted in any
form or by any means, electronic, mechanical, photocopying,
recording or otherwise, without the written permission of the
Institute of Personnel and Development, IPD House,
Camp Road, London, SW19 4UX.

Design by Paperweight
Typeset by The Comp-Room, Aylesbury
Printed in Great Britain by
The Cromwell Press, Wiltshire

British Library Cataloguing in Publication Data
A catalogue record for this book is available from the
British Library

ISBN 0-85292-693-6

The views expressed in this book are the author's own, and
may not necessarily reflect those of the IPD.

i)

**INSTITUTE OF PERSONNEL
AND DEVELOPMENT**

IPD House, Camp Road, London SW19 4UX
Tel: 0181 971 9000   Fax: 0181 263 3333
Registered office as above. Registered Charity No. 1038333
A company limited by guarantee. Registered in England No. 2931892

CONTENTS

ACKNOWLEDGEMENTS

This book gives many examples of how to undertake the suggested application building aspects. In doing so, the book refers to methods and techniques often associated with specific commercially available software. The author wishes to acknowledge the copyright of the software producers and their right to preserve their trademark. Where specific product references are made to such products as Microsoft Excel, Microsoft Access, Microsoft Office, Microsoft Word, Microsoft Powerpoint, Lotus 123, Quatro Pro, or any other commercially marketed product, it is as illustrations of the techniques suggested in this book. They represent an acknowledgement that the software referred to will be able to undertake the technique. No criticism of the products quoted is intended. The book's use of a software package name is not intended to reproduce the style or font of the trademark logo.

1

INTRODUCTION

Who is the book for?

This book will be of a wide appeal to anyone with an interest in developing ways to use data stored in a relational database. More specifically it is aimed at assisting

- HRM practitioners looking to develop their knowledge and abilities in utilising information technology within the management of the human resource
- students studying the practical uses of information technology in a management environment
- students studying for IPD professional examinations.

The need for the book

For a long time the HRM function has been criticised for not making enough use of the low-cost computer hardware and software that has become available in the marketplace. The author believes that there are several major reasons for the lack of uptake. Among these are:

- a reluctance to reduce individuals to a set of values
- a lack of knowledge of the abilities of software
- a belief that people decisions cannot be made by a computer
- an inability to use computerised databases and spreadsheets
- a fear of contravening the Data Protection legislation.

This book looks at ways that relatively inexpensive and

readily available software can be utilised within an HRM function, often utilising existing data that might have been stored on the staff records database.

Throughout the book examples are discussed and ways of using them suggested. The software used for examples is Microsoft Office Professional. All three of the major software packages within the Office suite will be used: MS Word, Excel 5 and Access 2. The examples are quoted in a form that can be utilised in any version of Microsoft Office Professional from 4.3 onwards. Most popular software can be used to undertake the suggested techniques within this book, but the database program used must be of the relational database type. (Relational databases are explained further in Chapter 2.)

The reader is not expected to be an expert in computer programming or even an expert operator: he or she will be coached through the techniques that could be used to achieve the suggested outcomes. Many readers will want to manage other people who will do the application development or the data loading required; this book will help the reader do this. The book is therefore written in a non-technical way, with no complex programming or program language code to try to understand. It is written by an author whose background has been in human resource management and employee development before moving into the academic environment to teach HRM at post-graduate level. As a result, the contents of the book are problem-based within the context of HRM, and not technically-based.

The author has been teaching and preaching the integration of the computer into the HRM function for many years. Indeed, as long ago as 1985 he developed and utilised a relational database application within the organisation that he worked for, to aid appraisal management and succession planning.

The philosophy of this book is encapsulated in the verb 'to aid'. The author does not, at the current time, believe that we should be looking at developing complex expert systems to make our HRM decisions for us. In fact, forthcoming European legislation may well be introduced to prevent that. The information produced by the PC should be used to enhance and improve the quality of decision-making on the part of the HRM staff. It is doubtful whether it is worth going to the expense of developing an expert system for a resource that is as dynamic and unpredictable as the human resource. (An expert system is one that is programmed to recognise a scenario or set of circumstances, and subsequently to make a decision on the best way forward.) The book therefore concentrates on using new ways to analyse data that probably already exists in one form or another within the organisation. What is suggested is that this data should be entered into a PC and managed in a different way, rather than as is so often the case stored passively in hard copy. The development of such a dynamic data store which is constantly evolving can be a considerable benefit in the contribution that HRM can make to the management of the overall business.

Topics covered

The author does not attempt to completely computerise the HRM function in this text. Indeed, setting up a staff records database is not an aim of the book. There are many software products on the market that can be used to do that. This book is more about how to utilise a computer in the management of the HRM function and to enhance its contribution.

Nor is it designed to be read from cover to cover. Each of the main chapters can be read as a separate entity – although it is recommended that Chapter 2 should be regarded as a basic text in order for the reader to become familiar with relational database modelling systems (RDBMS) and how to utilise them.

There are 10 major topic areas to be presented.

An introduction to database technology

This pivotal chapter of the book – which should be read for basic informative value – discusses and explains how a relational database can be constructed, how a database can be interrogated, and how links across the tables can be made. Although these are important features of the relational database, they would be of little use without being able to define how the resultant information should or could be presented. The chapter discusses presentation by examining the report facilities attached to databases. The structuring of reports is outlined here and throughout the subsequent chapters when specific requirements are addressed in the reports.

Implementing a computer application

It is always difficult to know what to computerise and what not to computerise. There is a temptation to try to get the computer to take on everything that it possibly could. In this chapter we look at deciding what to store and how best to store it. A decision how to store data is itself an important aspect of database technology, and one which may sometimes need careful thought.

It is often inferred that HRM lags behind in its utilisation of computerised information systems. Some of the possible reasons for this are discussed, and how such fears can be overcome. How to design an application for HRM is outlined, as is the prototyping methodology that can be used to aid the interface between user and computer. Finally, the chapter looks at the vital topic of system security, and how developers can seek to ensure that their application is safe from non-authorised users and from accidental corruption.

The recruitment process

The focus of this chapter is to discuss ways that the PC can enhance the recruitment process, help to present a professional image to the applicants, and reduce the amount of managerial time that has to be spent on the process. It also, of course, seeks to aid the finding of the right candidate for the job.

Managing the employment of staff

This chapter looks at the administration of the employment contract from start to finish and shows ways that ensure common approaches and behaviours can be achieved with employees – that ensure that things happen when they should and that employees get treated fairly. It also looks at job classification and evaluation.

The function of job evaluation and subsequent grading has met with varying degrees of popularity. This section illustrates a way that a simple job analysis scheme could be introduced via a database system that allows all jobs to be easily and fairly assessed against pre-defined criteria. Forthcoming

EU legislation regarding equal pay issues will require organisations to employ some method of measuring jobs against each other. This chapter shows how to institute such a system without turning it into an industry in itself.

The chapter goes on to examine salary management processes, and introduces a salary grade matrix module. It concludes with a look at the management of staff record systems.

Performance and development appraisal management

The appraisal process is often seen as a controversial area in personnel. This chapter looks at ways in which the process can be enhanced by using computerised systems to store the data. It shows how, through the development and use of performance rating and/or potential rating data, an organisation can monitor its staff development and the assessments made by its managers. Later chapters show how this data can be used in career management and succession-planning.

Job and managerial competencies

The chapter examines the concept of core competencies and looks at ways in which employees can be related to core and specific job competencies. It shows how skills gaps in the organisation can be identified for individuals, for departments, and for the whole organisation, thus leading to a training needs analysis. It looks at how data on competencies can be stored in a database in a way that it can be sensibly and most usefully employed by the organisation. A practical rather than a purist approach is adopted.

Succession-planning and career-planning

These are even more controversial topics in organisations than appraisal – yet a database can play an important part in helping managers to spot potential succession weaknesses in a business, or to reveal instances where staff may be blocked by one person's not performing as well as he or she might. The technique can also be a valuable aid to career management. By introducing one or two job parameters a picture can be built up of organisational risks in terms of insufficient succession to jobs.

Managing training and development

Simple techniques are detailed, such as the full use of word processing through to the production of training plans and budgets. The creation of a training record database is looked at as an example of the practical development of a standalone database (although it is probable that employees' individual records will contain details of training). Ways of evaluating training are also outlined. This is an area that is often under-utilised within HRM, yet can yield a great deal of information regarding the effective use of the training and development budget.

Modelling and budgeting

This chapter looks at the features of a spreadsheet and how a spreadsheet can be used to effectively model and control the budgeting process, even though the original data may well be extracted from a database. Spreadsheet programs are probably the most popular and powerful analysis tool commonly used by managers. Their appeal is in the use of powerful functions that allow sophisticated calculations to be made without having to resort to programming. This analytical ability is all the time being further developed by software manufacturers, making it easier for the user to arrive at answers to ever more complex problems.

Active use of the data

This final chapter looks at ways that the RDBMS can be used in areas that are less easy to format when the system is defined. It is certain that salary and reward structures will need to be modelled, but how it should be done is not always known in advance. Organisational priorities shift. The early reports in this chapter show how stored data can be extracted and used to model pay and reward systems relevant to the present or future of an organisation.

One of the most important duties that an employer is faced with is ensuring that fairness and equal opportunities occur in the workplace. It is difficult to do this in a fair way unless systems are in place to undertake actual monitoring. Throughout the book opportunities for ensuring or monitoring fairness, consistent management behaviour and equal opportunities are explored. In particular, methods for monitoring equal opportunities in the recruitment of staff, selection for training and development, payments and rewards, and promotional opportunities are examined. The information gathered in these areas is generated over a long period of time. Archiving is a particular strength of a computer and comes at a very low cost. What is more, the storage of data does not take up much room and it is always in the same place when a user goes looking for it. With some forethought in the setting up of a database system, it is surprising how much information can be extracted. A common expression regarding databases is that they are limited only by the imagination of the user or application builder. One of the objectives of this book is to help readers to open their minds and understand the power of relational databases so that they can utilise that power for themselves and their organisations. The chapter suggests ways that data relevant to equal opportunities incidents can be linked, extracted and reported upon in response to current events.

Data Protection

Since 1984, holders of data stored in an electronic form in the UK have been subject to regulation in accordance with the Data Protection Act. The Act requires that all such information holders and users must be registered with the Data Protection registrar.

The Act imposes a duty of care and disclosure of information held about data subjects, and is based on eight data principles:

1 Data must be obtained fairly and lawfully. This means that the supplier must be informed of the reason for the storage and use of the data.

2 The data may be used only for the specific purposes for which it was collected.

3 Disclosure of information to other people may be only to persons as described in the registration document.

4 Data must be relevant and adequate to satisfy the needs of the registered purpose.

5   The data held must be accurate and amended in order to be kept up to date.

6   The data must not be kept for longer than is necessary to achieve the requirements of the registered purpose.

7   The data subjects have the right to know what data is stored about them. They have the right to have it amended or erased if it is inaccurate.

8   Appropriate security procedures must be taken to avoid:

- unauthorised access to the data
- unauthorised alteration of the data
- unauthorised disclosure to third parties
- accidental loss of personal data.

From an HRM point of view the Act is designed to ensure that organisations who keep electronically stored information about its employees do so in a way that ensures data accuracy, and the legitimate use and disclosure of information held. There are few exceptions to the disclosure of data held. Generally an employee is entitled to a copy of the data held, whether that data represents fact or opinion about that person. Only data disclosure of which is considered to be prejudicial to the business need not be disclosed. Such prejudicial data might include data regarding succession plans for which there are possible contingencies for hypothetical circumstances. To disclose such information may well raise an employee's hopes of promotion that will cause demotivation if it does not come about, causing the employee perhaps to be less effective in the current role, or even to leave the business. This surely must be considered potentially prejudicial to the business.

In 1995 a European Union Directive (95/46/EC) was issued giving member states up to three years to pass legislation within their own countries that complies with the directive. Many of the requirements within the Directive are aimed at introducing legislation that covers aspects similar to those encased within the Data Protection Act already in force within Britain. There are some elements that are new to the UK, however, that will have to be introduced either by amending the current Act or introducing a new Act. According to the

Data Protection registrar, new elements will include

- the extension of Data Protection legislation to cover some manual records
- rules about the legitimacy of processing
- special rules for the processing of particularly sensitive personal data – data concerning racial or ethnic origin, political opinions, religious or philosophical beliefs, trade union membership, and data about health or sex life, criminal offences or convictions
- exemptions for personal data processed for journalistic, artistic or literary purposes to protect freedom of expression
- a duty on all 'controllers' (data users) to comply with Data Protection rules whether or not registered under the new system
- provisions designed to ensure that personal data being transferred to non-European Union countries will in general be adequately protected.

It remains to be seen how the British government will frame appropriate legislation. Some of the changes – notably the inclusion of some manual records – will have a considerable impact, as will the rules on the legitimacy of processing for some data storing purposes. From the HRM perspective it would appear that the Directive will increase professional and ethical requirements on the function. The Directive does not seek to prevent data about individuals from being stored, only to ensure that it complies with good practice when it is stored, and that it is consistently treated throughout the EU.

Commercial personnel record-keeping and HRM systems

If your organisation has a commercially produced human resource information system (HRIS), this book will help you to understand it and its capabilities more fully.

Although the book is written using standalone relational database examples, many of the commercially available HRIS do similar things. Some packages available on the market are specifically for HRM functions, such as career-planning: these are in effect standalone databases themselves. This book in no way attempts to suggest that such products are at all inferior or unable to undertake the applications suggested. Readers should explore the capabilities of their own systems, having read this book, to see if they can undertake the data analyses and derive the management reports that are proposed herein. Certainly, some of the more modern packages that may run in a Microsoft Windows environment may be flexible enough to undertake the requirements, as will systems specifically designed to undertake a function such as career planning. Some of the older systems, however, are less likely to be able to be adaptable enough to analyse the data in the way that is required. Even then, it is still likely that a user will be able to identify the data fields that are required and to export or download these to a separate file, often in a spreadsheet format. The file can then be read into other software packages.

Exporting data from a commercially produced application

If the data is exported in an Excel™ or Lotus 123™ format, it can be analysed in a spreadsheet, even though it might not be numerical data, for all modern spreadsheets have a simple database facility. The spreadsheet analysis of data may be all that is required. Chapters 11 and 12 outline some examples of using the spreadsheet functions to analyse data. It is an extremely powerful technique.

One of the benefits of extracting data from a database and analysing it in a spreadsheet is that having copied and saved the data in a file, the original data remains in the host application and cannot be corrupted or deleted while external analysis is going on. After exporting and manipulating the data, it is not usually possible – and certainly not desirable – to save the data back to the host application.

If your host application can export files, it might give you a choice of formats that the file may be exported in. Spreadsheet-file-format files are the most common. The application may well ask the user to make a choice. This choice could be selected by package name or by file extension. Package name is quite straightforward, but you may need to know the actual version number of the software that you are using. If you are exporting to a Windows-based package, whether a spreadsheet or a database, the version number of the Windows-based software can be found by clicking on the Help menu choice and selecting the About option.

If the application that you wish to export from asks for the file format by file extension, it requires the three characters that appear at the end of a file name after the full stop, which are put there automatically by the package. Lotus 123 files are defined as .WK followed by a character or number which will depend on the version of Lotus that you are using. Similarly, Excel has an extension .XL followed by another character or number, again depending on the version of the software in use. If your host database will export in a database format, it will either name the export formats available or ask for the extensions. Microsoft Access has the extension .MDB. Other databases have their own extensions: you should look them up in the program manual.

If the host database does not export in a database format, it need not be a problem. Most database packages will import a spreadsheet file and allow it to be treated as a database. So just export the file as, for example, an Excel 5 spreadsheet with an .XLS file extension.

There is one step that needs to be taken before importing the file from Excel 5 to Access 2 or any other compatible database.

As will be further explained in the next chapter, a database is divided into data fields, each of which has a unique name in the data table. When importing a file from a spreadsheet, the database package needs to identify each column of data with a field name. Before importing a file into the database, you therefore need to open it in the spreadsheet package and at the top of each column enter a short descriptor as the field name. It is best to keep it at fewer than eight characters and with no spaces because some databases do not accept long names with spaces.

As you go through the 'Import a file' routine the package will probably ask if the first value at the top of each column is to be regarded as the field name; select yes. Once opened as a database, the file can be saved as a database file. This will not delete the spreadsheet file – both can be used if desired, but if you do not wish to use the spreadsheet file it is probably best to delete it to save disk space and confusion. It can always be extracted again from the host database if necessary. Remember that when data is exported to another application it actually corresponds to a snapshot of the data as it was at the time of the export process. It will not change as new data is entered into the main database. It is therefore useful for analysis at the time of export, but new data should be downloaded for any future analysis.

If all of this seems a bit daunting, do not worry. You will only have to do it if you are exporting data. If you are setting up a database from scratch you need not bother with these actions.

Although this section has talked about commercially available personnel records software, many of the examples in the text are such that it is not necessary to enter them into a personnel record system. Managing the recruitment process, for example, would certainly not need data to be entered into the personnel record system. In this case we will look at ways of developing a standalone management system.

2

RELATIONAL DATABASES

What is a database?

A computerised database is a way of structuring and storing data in a table in such a way that the data can be manipulated and interrogated by the user to turn it from basic stored data to meaningful information in respect of a question or query posed by the user. The stored data can be in numerical form, but it is more normally stored in alphanumeric character or text form.

This is the main difference between a spreadsheet and a database. In a spreadsheet, the user enters numbers into cells and then performs calculations on those numbers using mathematical formulae ranging from the very simple to the very complex, depending on the user's needs and abilities.

The reader may be thinking that text can be entered into a spreadsheet – and this is true – but the text that is entered is usually in the form of headings and labels, and does not play a part in the calculations. It is passive data, whereas the data entries in a database are dynamic and can be used to resolve queries and produce reports.

It is possible to use most spreadsheets as record-keeping databases – but this is actually to use the package as a database and not as a spreadsheet. For the purposes of this chapter let us accept that spreadsheet packages such as Excel and Lotus 123 are primarily for numerical input and calculations.

Probably the simplest form of database that most people use is a table of the names and addresses of people they write to. Many people have this stored within their word processors as a mail merge file. It is a good illustration to use as an explanation of a database table. Table 1 shows a list of the types of

Table I

DETAILS DATA TABLE
TITLE
FORENAME
SURNAME
ROAD
TOWN
POSTCODE
PHONE

data that you might want to store in a mail merge file. The purpose of storing this data in a separate file is that it only has to be entered once and can then be merged into a current document. This has at least two benefits: the user does not have to re-type addresses, which is particularly useful when sending the same letter or memo to lots of different people, and the user does not have to spend time looking up addresses that may be stored in a hard-copy filing system somewhere.

How does the database know what data is what?

Clearly, each entry in a database table is going to be different. The name and address of one recipient of a standard letter is obviously going to be different from that of the next recipient. To make sense of the data that has been entered, the computer has to be able to classify the data and enter it into its memory in a way that it can retrieve it so that it makes sense. To achieve this, the data is broken up into sections called data fields. Look back at Table 1: it shows the data field names that could be used to store the details of the people in the mail merge list.

Although the details of each person are different, the type of data stored is the same. For example, each person has a 'Title', 'Forename', 'Surname', 'Road', 'Town', 'Postcode' and 'Phone number'. This is the key to how the database can make sense of the data. The database can be thought of as a matrix of cells: Figure 1 shows such a matrix.

Each column is headed with the field name that is the identifier for the type of data that is stored in that column. The individual data for each entrant is entered in a row until a full input of data for each item is entered. Each row of data is known as a data record. Look at the matrix in Figure 1 and it can be seen that all of the data fields that contain the surnames are in the third column. All of the details that refer to Philip Wright are in the second row. This second row is the data record for Philip Wright.

Figure 1

TITLE	FORENAME	SURNAME	ROAD	TOWN	POSTCODE	PHONE
MR	THOMAS	JONES	6 ALBANY ST	CARDIFF	CD3 RT5	01234 567890
MR	PHILIP	WRIGHT	5 HIGH ST	DUNDEE	DU4 R5T	01564 265987
MS	ANN	SMITH	3 LOWER RD	NORWICH	NR7 T8R	01874 357451
MRS	JOSIE	TUNNY	12 ACACIA RD	DOVER	DV8 T9W	01896 145872
MR	FRED	WINTER	23 BELL RD	EXETER	EX3 6YH	01698 258463
MISS	JANE	GREEN	34 RING ROAD	LONDON	SW25 T6Y	01589 254189

THIS IS A
DATABASE

– FIELDS GO DOWN
IN COLUMNS

– RECORDS GO
ACROSS IN ROWS

Data integrity

Having established that a database table consists of data fields and data records, there is one further important feature that needs to be understood about the way that a database program manages itself. Without it the reliability of the data could not be guaranteed. Once data has been entered into a record, the programme must always store that record as a whole record so that the same forename always relates to the same surname. Philip Wright must always be associated with the address that has been entered for him or the application would be useless. This feature of the database is known as retaining database integrity. It ensures that data fields will always relate to the same data record in which they were originally entered. The user is given the ability to deliberately change, delete or update data, usually by overtyping the original, but the system cannot be, and is not given, any ability to mix up the data fields. Having made the point about the importance of data integrity, it is not necessary to dwell further on the subject: the process is undertaken and managed by the software program automatically, and the user need not worry about it. It is sufficient to accept that the data will retain integrity without the user's having to do anything.

Manipulating data

So far all that is contained in the database table is a copy of the list that has been typed in. That's fine if it is part of a mail merge table and you need to send a letter to everyone – but if that is not the requirement, then we need to be able to manipulate the data.

Manipulating data in a database is really very easy. There are several ways that it can be done. One of the most common things that has to be done with lists of personal data is to put them into alphabetical order by surname. Anyone who has had to do this task manually, perhaps to produce a list of all employees in alphabetical order, by department and by location, will know how tedious and time-consuming this can be. With a computerised database it could not be simpler: what can take a long time to do manually can be achieved with a computer in seconds. Even a data table of many hundreds of records can be sorted in seconds. Whatever software program is being used it will have a data sort function. Initiating this process will probably lead to the appearance of a dialogue box on the screen seeking some information from the user. In a simple sort system the program will need to know which data field the user wishes to sort by. This is usually best achieved by using primary and secondary data fields. Thus it is possible to ask the application to sort the records in ascending or descending order by using the Surname data field as a primary sort field, and to further sort the list by using the Forename field as a secondary sort field, thereby causing Alan Smith to appear in the list before Amanda Smith.

Querying data

As well as putting data into alphabetical order, it may be that the requirement is to extract some records and leave others in the table. Suppose that the need is to find all of the people in the database that live in a particular town. The way to achieve this is to 'Query' the database. Just as all databases can perform sorts, so all databases can perform 'Query' actions. Some will be capable of more sophisticated query techniques than others, but all will do the simple type that is outlined here.

What actually happens when a query action is performed is that the data records that fit the criteria being requested are copied into a temporary answer table. The original data entries are not touched and will therefore not be corrupted as a result of the query process.

A typical query routine asks the user to identify the data field or fields that the query is to be based on, usually by showing a representation of the data table as in Table 2. The user then types in the required criteria and the program sorts through the data table that is being interrogated and produces an answer table. By typing 'London' in the criteria cell of the 'Town' data field, all data records of people who live in London will be extracted and placed in the answer table. This answer data table, can then be used as the basis of a report or mail merge so that letters can be sent to all the people on the list that fit the query criteria.

The answer table is known as a volatile table – that is, it is not retained when the user exits the program or when another query is asked. A new table becomes the answer table and overwrites the former answer table.

If the user wishes to keep an answer table, it will need to be renamed and stored. However, it is more likely that the user will store the query rather than the table it produces, and then just run the query on the data table whenever it is needed. This method has several advantages over the renaming and storing of a data table. Once queried and stored, the table is static and contains information that will soon become out of date; the table will take up more memory space than the query; and, most importantly, by storing and running the query the resultant information will always be based on the current data stored in the main data table. Any entries that have been made since the last time the query was used will therefore be included in the interrogation and in the new answer table if they fit the criteria.

Queries can become quite complex and set criteria for more

than one data field in the table. Suppose it became necessary to find all females with surnames starting with the letter 'H' or letters after 'H' in the alphabet who live in Norwich. A data query as shown in Table 2 could be used.

Some of the criteria requirements probably need to be explained. They are typical query parameters that will be used by a database. Although they are quite logical, they are not necessarily what the user might immediately think of as the way to ask the question.

The first requirement was to find females. The data in the table does not actually contain gender details – but by thinking about it we can see that logically anyone in the list who does not have the title of Mr will by default be female. Such logic would not work if we had titles like Dr or Prof but for the purpose of this example it illustrates an important feature

Table 2

TITLE	FORENAME	SURNAME	ROAD	TOWN	POSTCODE	PHONE
NOT "MR"		>G*		=NORWICH		

of database interrogation. It is often easier to ask the question in a way that is the reverse of how we would normally think. It may take some getting used to this concept, but some examples later in the chapter will reinforce the idea. For instance, it will be seen that the quickest way to find the number of current employees is to count all the employees that have not left yet.

The next criteria requirement in the query is to list all people with a surname that starts with 'H' or higher in the alphabet. The query achieves this by using the entry ' >G*'. The > symbol is the mathematical symbol denoting 'greater than'. By using this, the database will produce any surname commencing with any alphabetical letter that comes after 'G' in the alphabet but not including G. The * following the capital G denotes that any combination of letters or symbols that follows the first letter greater than G should be shown. Without this character the database query would literally search for any single-letter surname of H and above. Unless there were any single-letter entries it would give a nil return.

The final task for this query is to confine the search to data records of people living in Norwich. This is straightforward enough – except for one thing that needs to be mentioned. The database query is a literal query: it will only match to the exact pattern of the criterion parameter. If there is a mis-spelling in the query, the database program will not know and will search for a match to the misspelled criterion. Similarly, if there is a misspelled entry in the data records (eg Norich), it will not be picked up by a literal search.

Some database packages allow for query searches to include criteria that are not absolutely literal by accepting the use of a term such as 'LIKE' Norwich. The program will then match close spellings or phonetically similar entries to Norwich. Beware: it might pick out Northwich, which is not what is required, so check the answer if using 'LIKE' searches.

Relational databases

The previous sections have outlined some of the basic con-cepts of how a data record-keeping system works. This type of database is useful for storing unrelated lists of data like record collections or an address list; it is not as useful for storing such data as employee records. The problem with the two dimensional database that has been outlined is that each time something new happens, all of the data has to be re-entered about the item or person as well as the event. A simple exam-ple would be keeping attendance data on a database. In the two-dimensional example used so far, all of the details of an employee would have to be entered each time the person was absent; name, job title, location, and the details of the absence and its duration. Clearly, this is not only time-consuming but, from a technical viewpoint, it is a waste of available memory space. To overcome this problem the concept of the relational database modelling systems (RDBMS) has been developed. The concept is quite simple but the reality leads to an ability to store data in a simpler form with less input – and, more importantly, it leads to the ability to ask queries that link data that at the time of entry may have seemed unconnected.

The fundamental feature of a relational database modelling

system is that data can be stored in different tables but linked across from table to table in order to extract information from the data. It is said that a RDBMS is limited only by the imagination of the application developer. This is probably a bit of an exaggeration – but it is mainly true.

A relational database stores data related to specific events or sets of data in distinct tables. Each of these events or sets of information can be identified as an occurrence. They are often described as an object. Each object should contain only the data required to store the occurrence of one unique event. The data relating to each event is entered into a data table that is specifically set up to store that data and nothing else.

Table 3 shows two data tables: one for storing the name and address of an employee, and the other for storing data about absences. These two tables can be linked or merged by linking two data fields with the same information in them – for example, the surname – and extracting the name and address from the details table and the absence durations and the reason for absence from the attendance table. The result is an answer table that has merged the two source tables together and extracted the required data fields – as shown in Table 4.

The advantage of entering data into tables such as these is that the name and address details need only to be entered in the address table once. The details for the absences need only the name and the absence details entered for each absence, and not the address.

However, in the way that these tables are set up and the way that the link is made, it cannot be known with any certainty that the same Joneses are linked in the answer. It can be seen in Table 4 that Carol Jones' details have also been printed together with an absence. The problem with this whole answer table is that the integrity of the data cannot be guaranteed. The reason for this is that the link of surname is ambiguous: there may be many people with the surname Jones (or any other surname may be duplicated, for that matter). So it is necessary to make the links between the tables unique to the person for whom the entry is being made.

Table 3

DETAILS DATA TABLE
TITLE
FORENAME
SURNAME
ROAD
TOWN
POSTCODE

ATTENDANCE TABLE
FORENAME
SURNAME
ABSENCE DATE
DURATION
REASON CODE

A common way to achieve this is to give each employee a unique number. Every time data is to be entered into the system concerning a person, his or her unique identifying employee number must be entered. This is not as troublesome as it sounds. In fact, it makes life simpler.

Look at Figure 2 (page 22). A new data field has been added to each data table, both incorporating the field name of employee number. This number can be nominated by the system or it could be the employee's company number. (Avoid using National Insurance numbers because they are long and cumbersome to type in, leaving room for error.) Once the employee details data record has been entered into the table, all other tables can link to it to get the employee details any time they are required. This means that when entering details about other occurrences in other tables, only the employee identifier has to be entered. The name is not needed. In Figure 2 it can be seen that the name of the individual is never entered – only the number. From this data a query can be posted that links the two tables and extracts a report which gives the personal details once and then lists the absences. Using this technique is to be preferred: input time is cut down and memory requirement is kept to a minimum. It also allows the system to run faster.

Table 4

TITLE	FORENAME	SUR-NAME	ROAD	TOWN	ABSENCE DATE	DURATION	REASON
MR	THOMAS	JONES	6 ALBANY ST	CARDIFF	10/1/97	5	SICK
MR	THOMAS	JONES	6 ALBANY ST	CARDIFF	1/3/97	10	HOLS
MR	THOMAS	JONES	6 ALBANY ST	CARDIFF	15/3/97	5	SICK
MRS	CAROL	JONES	4 BERRY RD	CARLISLE	3/2/97	4	HOLS

Readers may be groaning at this time that they will have to remember the employee number of each employee. That is not the case. The database application can be prompted to give the number of an employee, or the number can be entered onto the hard copy report form that is used as an input document.

Using the employee identification number for associating data input with individuals means that data can be checked to ensure that the right person is being used to link to. An application can easily be made to confirm the personal details of the holder of the number as soon as the number is entered; operators can be asked to confirm that this is the right person before any further entry is made.

It must be understood that an employee number cannot be re-used for a different person when an employee leaves a company. Although Data Protection legislation would preclude us from keeping personal details for long after the employment, other data may be useful for ongoing reporting of statistics and trends. Once the ability to personally identify an individual has been removed, the original employee number may still retain its role as the link between tables.

Deciding the structure of tables

From the above it can be seen that tables containing lots of data fields are not necessary – indeed, they are not desirable. The smaller the number of data fields, the easier it is to input data and to make links across tables.

Table 5 starts to show how an employee record system can be built up using the features of a RDBMS. It is not part of the intention of this book to discuss the attributes of an overall

Figure 2

DETAILS DATA TABLE	ATTENDANCE TABLE
EMPLOYEE NUMBER ◄──────►	EMPLOYEE NUMBER
TITLE	
FORENAME	
SURNAME	ABSENCE DATE
ROAD	DURATION
TOWN	REASON CODE
POSTCODE	

Table 5

DETAILS DATA TABLE		ATTENDANCE TABLE
EMPLOYEE NUMBER		EMPLOYEE NUMBER
TITLE		
FORENAME		
SURNAME		ABSENCE DATE
DATE OF BIRTH		DURATION
START DATE WITH COMPANY		REASON CODE
GENDER		
LEAVE DATE		

JOB DETAILS DATA TABLE		CONTRACT DETAILS TABLE
EMPLOYEE NUMBER		CONTRACT TYPE
JOB TITLE		HOURS
LOCATION		SICK DAYS ENTITLEMENT
DEPARTMENT		HOLIDAY DAYS ENTITLEMENT
START DATE IN JOB		PENSION RATE
CONTRACT TYPE		
GRADE		
GRADE POINT		

ADDRESS DETAILS		PHONE NUMBERS
		EMPLOYEE NUMBER
EMPLOYEE NUMBER		DATE
DATE OF ENTRY		HOME PHONE
ADDRESS 1		FAX NUMBER
ADDRESS 2		MOBILE NUMBER
TOWN		PAGER NUMBER
COUNTY		
POST CODE		

personnel record-keeping system – but for illustrative purposes it is useful to discuss concepts that many readers will
be familiar with.

Table 5 consists of six tables that would undoubtedly be
usable in a commercial application in a form similar to that
shown. There are some changes in data fields to those which
have been used thus far. For example, the details table no
longer has details of the employee's home address in it. This
is because the address may well change and we would want to
keep a record of the previous address. The data required in the
present details table will not change (with the possible exception of the surname in the case of marriage, a circumstance it
is not necessary to explore further at this time). It is sufficient
to accept that all of the data entry requirements for the details

field will only ever need to be entered into the system once. This is therefore a table of unique data that will identify an employee for the rest of the system. As far as the system is concerned, this is the master table: it is the set of data which holds the key information about an employee number. This will be the first table to have data entered into it when initiating an employment. The first data entry will be that of the employee number, which may itself be generated by the system. This is the primary or key data field and is set up so that a duplicate number or code cannot be entered into this table. As a result, it will be possible to distinguish between two employees who have the same name – they will have different employee numbers. It is also possible to be assured that the integrity of the database will be maintained. There can only be one entry in this table for a person, so that any other tables linked to this table by a common employee number must link to only one record. It is crucial that the reader grasps this concept at this time.

All of the other tables of data can be permitted to have more than one entry for each employee number. This is how a historical reporting system can be built up. Look at Table 5. The details table gives the unique personal information about an employee. This is then linked to the job details table. There could be a number of entries in this table for an employee. Note that the employee details table has a start-date with company field. The job details table also has a date data field, but this relates to the date the employee started in the current job. By linking these two tables we can quickly find out about an employee's job history within the company, and by running a query that also includes a calculation we can see the overall length of service and the length of service in each position held. This is a simple but useful example of how tables can be meaningfully linked. Further links could be made to other tables. There is no theoretical limit to the number of tables that can be linked in the database – but practice shows that too many links will slow the machine down and often cause a nil answer to emerge, because some of the queries may conflict with each other. However, for the purposes of this book it is unlikely that the number of links with other tables will cause problems.

Links of up to five or six tables will probably be sufficient.

Building on the job record query example: if the job details table is linked to the absence details table, it is possible to get a record of employee absence for an employee for each job held in the organisation since he or she was first employed. So if an employee developed a poor attendance record it would be possible to pin down when it occurred and in which job.

Any meaningful data can be linked across tables: the link does not have to be the employee number, nor does it have to be the same link for the whole query.

Figure 3 (page 26) shows the links that could be made between four tables. Having established these links by telling the system which data fields link with each other, it is possible to extract any data fields from the database that are required.

Suppose that for each employee it was necessary to identify the cost of absence, by department, by location. Without the data stored in the database it would take forever to achieve this; an organisation probably would not bother. It may be possible to get the data from a payroll system, but that would probably mean waiting and paying for the report production. Look at Figure 3 and see how five tables can be linked to produce data that a report could be assembled from to give the required information.

The details, attendance and job details tables are linked via the employee number data field. But the job details field is also linked to the contract details table and the pay scales table. By extracting the information relating to an employee, employee number, name and forename (employee details table), number of days sick since start of financial year for each employee (attendance table), grouping these by department and location (job details table) identifying the maximum paid sick days (contract details table) and getting the salary earned by each employee (pay scale table), a query answer table could be formed. This could be saved as a new table and a scheme developed which would undertake the necessary calculations to produce the reports. Reports will be outlined later in this chapter. The data outlined here could in fact be exported from the database to a spreadsheet where further analysis might be easier to undertake, particularly if it was an isolated analysis that would not need to be repeated.

Figure 3

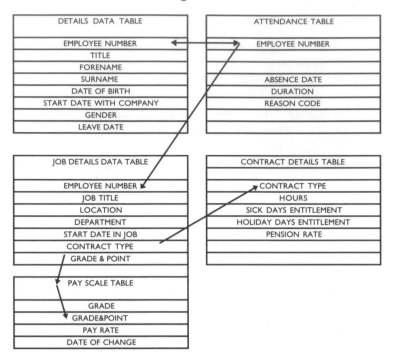

This is a good time to take a break or to go back over the explanation of how data tables can be linked or related to each other.

Deciding what data field types to use

Data fields were discussed earlier in the chapter. There are some other points that need to be borne in mind when deciding what data fields to put into a data table. An RDBMS can store data in different formats, which makes it easier for the stored data to be used and ensures that unsuitable data cannot be entered into the field. A good example of this field formatting is numerical data. If when the database is being designed it is known that an entry into a field will always be numerical, it is best to format the field as such. By doing this, calculations can be performed on the data using formulae and functions similar to those used in a spreadsheet. If the field were not formatted as a numerical field, the possible calculations would be limited and might not be possible at all. If trying to undertake calculations on a non-numeric data field, the system may return an incompatible data type error.

Another format that can be used is a date format. By nominating the field as a date-only field, date calculations can be performed. The way that dates are stored by a database is to give them a chronological numerical value from date day one, which represents 1 January 1900. Each day is then assigned a value calculated from day òne, so that 36,525 will be 31 December 1999. By storing dates in this numerical form, it is very easy for a database application to make calculations on dates using standard arithmetical and algebraic logic.

A person's actual age should therefore never be entered as a data field; only the date of birth. If an employee's date of birth is 1 January 1966, this may be entered as such by the operator. The computer will invisibly translate the date – provided that the field has been formatted as a date field – into a number (in this case, 24,108). If on 30 November 1998 a report of employees' ages is required, a report with a calculated field (today minus date of birth) will be compiled. The computer knows that it needs to subtract 24,108 from 36,129, which equals 12,021. A quick calculation by the computer shows that the employee is currently 32 years old. Once a report is set up to undertake this calculation on all of the employees in the organisation, it can be saved as a named report and run at any time. Because the report is working on date fields based on 'today', the calculations will always show the current age. The same principle can also be used for identifying length of service with a company, or to flag up when an employee has ten years' service or is one year away from standard retirement age. All of this and more can be derived from the simple entry of date of birth or start date with company. Other chapters will show the entry of dates of events to be very important when reporting management decision-making information. Each host database will have different types of data fields. Thought needs to be given to the format for each field. If a field can be formatted as a data field type, it should be, rather than being left as a default text field.

Data input

One of the problems that the reader may have perceived is
that if data is stored in small tables that are linked only by an
employee number, data input may be a little awkward.
Without planning the input, that may well be the case – but
with logical thought and planning, inputting data need not be
a problem.

The first data that is entered into the system about an
employee must be, and logically will be, his or her personal
details. Sensibly, sickness and absence details will only ever
be entered for an employee already on the system. The personal details of an individual will therefore always be available for viewing when entering data: this will ensure that the
right person is having data entered about him or her. All systems do this differently but most systems allow the person
inputting data to call up the individual input form to the
screen and then allow either the department, individual name
or employee number to be entered or searched for.
Applications running in Microsoft Windows will allow the
user to scroll down a list of individuals and choose the correct
person for whom details can be entered. This means that only
bona fide employee numbers will be used. Of course there is
no absolute guarantee that the information gets entered
against the right employee, but all systems build in some
safeguards to ensure that this eventuality is minimised.

The way that systems control input is to develop a series of
legitimate input procedures or occurrences. For example,
there will be a new starter procedure. By entering this procedure, an operator will be prompted for the required data and
the system will also make checks on the validity of the data.
In an employee record system, for instance, it is unlikely that
the system would accept dates of birth that meant that the
employee was under 16 or over 65. The employee number
would also be validated against a pre-defined format to see
that it was not a duplicate number. If this number was not
actually generated by the system, it is likely that the operator
would be asked to key the number in twice during the routine
to check against input typing errors. The operator might also
be asked to verify the number displayed on the screen, since
the inputting of a wrong employee number at this stage would

render latter inputs meaningless and void. Indeed, a well designed system would reject data entered against a different, invalid number. Once the primary data has been entered onto the system, all of the other routines can be undertaken. These routines will include data entry procedures for attendance recording, performance recording, grading, job details, etc.

Assigning data to an employee

Each of these routines will require the individual employee to be identified and probably the date of the entry. By creating an input form on screen for each of these routines which will allow the employee name and number to be shown together with the job title and location, it need only be a matter of accepting system prompts to enter the employee number and the date when entering individual occurrence data such as absence and absence reason data. In some cases it is even possible for the system to show a picture of the employee, thus further minimising the risk of misentry (provided the person inputting knows the person). The screen will contain details from at least two tables, perhaps more. This chapter has shown how the data is stored in small object tables in order to facilitate comprehensive analysis of the data. The reader will have realised that in order to get the employee details onto the screen in an identifiable format the key data of surname, forename, employee number and current job title, location and department would have to be extracted from different tables. This extraction would be invisible to the user of the system. More important is the requirement for seamless input. In the case of absence recording this is not too much of a problem because the input data would be going to only one table. Nevertheless, the input process can be made as easy as possible: the system can enter the current employee number into the attendance table, and the system can work out the number of days of absence from the start of absence to the return from absence. A small subprogramme or macro will need to be developed to allow for a five-day working week from any concurrent days of absence that include a weekend or other nominated days. Alternatively, the operator could enter the number of days – but this is not a sophisticated technique: it is open to error and it is trying to do what computers do best – iterative calculations.

Where an input routine needs to put data into more than one table, the input form technique is of great value. If, for example, an employee review screen was being used that identified the current findings of an appraisal, the screen might ask for date, performance assessment, potential assessment, and development needs. This data would certainly need to be stored in more than one table: performance and potential assessment in one table, and development needs in another. By using a form screen and nominating which tables need which data, it will only be necessary to put the date in once, and the employee details will be taken from the screen without input being necessary.

The principal requirement of data input is to be as simple as possible for the inputting person to achieve. This includes the layout and colour scheme of the screen. The human–computer interface is a complex issue. One major aspect to bear in mind is that screens should be kept as constant in layout as possible. Input screens should have the employee look-up details always in the same place, input fields in the same area of the screen, a consistent and relaxing colour scheme, and a prominent screen title or purpose. When considering screens for other purposes – such as output or report information – a different, but again constant, format should be used for each type of transaction. A similar layout is useful with a different colour depicting report output: in this way the user gets to know instinctively if he or she is in the right area of the application.

Output reports

Output reports from a computer database are the most powerful and useful aspect of the HR database system. Without an ability to produce selective and/or calculated reports from the data input into the system, the whole thing is nothing more than a passive electronic filing system. There are many organisations that use HR systems as little else. One of the purposes of this book is to allow the reader an insight into the possibilities of a database of related data. For example: in a passive or manual system it is possible to log holidays against individuals, and it is relatively easy then to check an individual's holiday taken against total holidays to be taken. But with a RDBMS it is possible to ask the machine to perform calculations on the data entered that might be too time-consuming to do manually or on a non-relational database, or just might not be possible at all.

Using the holiday details example, we can explore the concept of system-generated reports. One of the problems that is often encountered by HR managers in a business is that of employees' seeking to carry holiday entitlement over from one holiday year to the next. Many organisations do not allow this or limit it to a few days; some, of course, have no guidelines. Often the first that anyone knows of the problem, except the employee and the immediate boss, is when the employee seeks payment for the days outstanding. Some organisations allow this; others do not. The rights and wrongs are not expanded upon here, except to say that for payment to be allowed can play havoc with the budget and forecast for the coming year if holidays for the previous year are having to be bought off. A non-financial argument is that if time could not be found for the year's holiday during the holiday year, how is it going to be found in the next holiday year in addition to the entitlement for that year?

Enough moralising – let us consider what the RDBMS can do to assist the organisation to manage the system. There are a number of ways in which the data could be input into the system. The most likely is for the main entries to be stored in the attendance table. Depending on the level of sophistication required, data can be entered against a code of 'H' for holiday taken and 'PH' for proposed holiday. This depends on whether or not the organisation has a mechanism for easily inputting the data (it is not the purpose of the author to lose sight of reality and expect every minor detail to be put into a computer). Supposing, however, that these two types of data were input into the system, a number of management reports could be easily produced. A useful feature about reports is that they can be set up once and then run off either on a regular basis or as and when required. They can of course be prepared in an *ad hoc* fashion by the system user to help solve a particular problem of the moment at any time.

Our database now includes all of the details of the employees: where they work, by department, location, grade, salary, job type and contract type; who they report to, start date with the company, etc., and of course the proposed holiday dates and the actual holiday dates.

The data types listed above are stored in many different tables, but in most cases they can all be linked via the employee number.

From the data listed above any number of reports can be produced. We may look at just a few which illustrate the types of link that can be made. In its simplest form a report is a listing of data which is grouped in some way that is useful and which summarises the data that has been input into the system. A list of all holidays booked would be such a list. This is simply a listing by location and department of all employees who have booked holidays. Look at Table 6. This report has its uses. It can immediately be seen that two people from the same department have booked their holidays at exactly the same time – information useful in helping the manager decide whether such a situation is practical.

This simple report could be made to give much more information without too much additional work. The report is set out by location and department, but it tells us only who has booked holidays – it does not tell us who has not, and it does not give details of employees' entitlement. These embellishments can be simply added, together with a calculation of any entitlement of days left or whether any employees have exceeded their allowance.

In Table 7 (page 34) these additions have been made. It can now be seen that one employee has not yet booked any holiday, and one has booked three days more than her entitlement. If allowed at all, it should actually be recorded in the system as an authorised unpaid absence. Clearly, this example only represents a very small department. The good part about preparing a report format for a database, however, is that it is only necessary to develop the structure of the report for one iteration of the grouping. So although this particular illustration shows only one department in one location, the computer system would actually produce a report that listed all locations, all departments at each location, and all employees in each department.

A variation on this report could be produced as a location/department report in percentage of holidays booked or taken against the holiday year. The level of reporting required depends on the recipient of the report, as does the format. Table 8 (page 35) shows at a glance how an HR manager could see how the holidays taken and booked were progressing against the amount of the year remaining. It has to be borne in mind that holidays peak at certain times, and the percentage comparison should only be seen as a guide. It can nevertheless be seen in the example that there is a problem in the finance department which, left alone, may cause employees to become disgruntled if they lose their entitlement. This is not to suggest that it is the responsibility of the HRM department to ascertain holiday dates or even to manage the process. It is, however, down to the HRM department to see that the human resource within the organisation is effectively managed by the organisation. Reports of this nature that make calculations based on input data are an invaluable way of helping to ensure that this purpose is achieved.

The value of the report output from the system is in its ability to undertake calculations on the data and to make

Table 6

LOCATION	GLASGOW		REPORT	DATE	1/1/98
DEPARTMENT	SALES				
emp no:	forename	surname	start date	return date	hol days
1234	JOHN	SMITH	1/6/98	15/6/98	10
1234	JOHN	SMITH	5/9/98	12/9/98	5
				EMPLOYEE SUB TOTAL	15
1356	SALLY	PRESTON	7/7/98	21/7/98	10
1356	SALLY	PRESTON	11/11/98	30/11/98	13
				EMPLOYEE SUB TOTAL	23
2679	BRIAN	PHELPS	7/7/98	21/7/98	10
2679	BRIAN	PHELPS	16/8/98	23/8/98	5
2679	BRIAN	PHELPS	15/10/98	18/10/98	3
				EMPLOYEE SUB TOTAL	18
				DEPT TOTAL	56

links that otherwise would be difficult. For instance: if an organisation did have a problem with holiday dates, a report could even be drawn up that analysed the problem by manager rather than by department. This might throw a clearer light upon the problem.

It is not possible in this or any other book to outline all of the different types of report that could be obtained. The purpose of this section has been to demonstrate how links are made between data tables in order to extract data and to turn it into management information as the basis for making decisions. Data can be linked, grouped and calculated upon – even calculated data that does not exist as input data can be further calculated upon. For example: an overall departmental salary

Table 7

LOCATION	GLASGOW		REPORT	DATE	1/1/98
DEPARTMENT	SALES				
emp no:	forename	surname	start date	return date	hol days
1234	JOHN	SMITH	1/6/98	15/6/98	10
1234	JOHN	SMITH	5/9/98	12/9/98	5
				SUB TOTAL	15
				ENTITLED	20
				BALANCE	5
1356	SALLY	PRESTON	7/7/98	21/7/98	10
1356	SALLY	PRESTON	11/11/98	30/11/98	13
				SUB TOTAL	23
				ENTITLED	20
				BALANCE	-3
2679	BRIAN	PHELPS	7/7/98	21/7/98	10
2679	BRIAN	PHELPS	16/8/98	23/8/98	5
2679	BRIAN	PHELPS	15/10/98	18/10/98	3
				SUB TOTAL	18
				ENTITLED	20
				BALANCE	2
2348	JANE	FELLOWS			0
				ENTITLED	20
				BALANCE	20
				TOTAL BOOKED	56
				TOTAL LEFT	24
				EXCEEDED DAYS	3

Table 8

REPORT DATE	31/7/98	% OF YEAR GONE	58%
LOCATION	GLASGOW		
DEPARTMENT	% HOLS BOOKED	% HOLS TAKEN	± OF % OF HOL YEAR ELAPSED
SALES	95%	38%	-20%
PRODUCTION	75%	50%	-8%
MARKETING	100%	75%	+17%
FINANCE	40%	30%	-28%
CARLISLE			
DISTRIBUTION	100%	72%	+14%
ADMIN	90%	65%	+7%

bill which is calculated by adding all salaries could then be further calculated to discover the monthly overall salary or the average salary per employee. Some programs will do this at the report stage and some at the query stage. Whichever – it is still a simple task for a RDBMS . . . but one that would take a very long time to achieve manually.

Later chapters will explore the ways in which the PC-based relational database might aid the HR department to achieve its role effectively in specific areas. It is hoped that readers will then be able to develop their own use of a computer further within their own organisations.

This chapter may have taken some time to absorb – but it is the mainstay of the rest of the book if the reader is not used to RDBMS techniques.

3

IMPLEMENTING A

COMPUTERISED APPLICATION

Deciding what to store and how to store it

There is a distinct danger that too much data might be stored in a relational database modelling system (RDBMS), thus causing it to become a law enforcement system rather than a management aid. Chapter 2 has shown that it is possible to make links between stored data that allow questions to be asked which would never have been possible in the past. The system developer and specifier must take care not to get carried away, to keep the whole process in perspective. The benefit of a RDBMS is that it can be expanded at any time in the future. As long as new tables can be linked to employee details or other identifiers, new data can be utilised within an application.

To give an example of this temptation to store too much, let us suppose that our RDBMS included employee details and details of a company car scheme. It is logical that this should be so, and from this data we can quickly see who is responsible for which car, etc. But there may also be a temptation to keep a data table that stores details of petrol purchases, especially if the organisation uses fuel credit cards to purchase fuel. While on the face of it this might appear to be sensible – and in some organisations it may be – it is more likely either that such details will be held by the finance department or, in the case of fuel credit cards, that the card organisation will undertake analyses of miles per gallon and overall purchase on the client company's behalf. To store such data in an HRM database would therefore probably be double accounting and/or an expensive input exercise that yields little or no new information. It is therefore important that the purpose of the departmental objectives be adhered to, and the temptation to input data – either because it can be done or because of aspirations to play Big Brother – should be avoided. This said, it must be recognised that in some organisations such uses of the system may well be legitimate and should therefore be undertaken. Only the organisations themselves can make such decisions.

One further issue that it does raise, however, is that of compatibility between systems. The point has been made that other departments will be storing data for their own purposes, and the example quoted was the finance department's logging fuel purchases by employee. Suppose that one vehicle came up with consistently high mileage figures or high fuel consumption: it would be useful if the finance system and the HRM system had some way that they could be linked. In the case of a RDBMS this is perfectly possible, provided some sensible link could be made between the tables.

The process of making the link would involve exporting data from either system and importing it to the other system. Most systems allow for import and export. If in this case the importing system was the HRM system, the likely link would be via the vehicle registration number. That would be held in the HRM system data table on the vehicle details – and in the same table would be the employee number. By linking the imported fuel purchased table to the vehicle details and then to the employee details table, we can thus quickly identify who is the registered company driver.

There are many other links that can also be made and that would be relevant for different situations in relation to this example. The RDBMS should confine itself to storing appropriate data and not double-account either within itself or with other organisational systems. A user should ensure that the systems can be linked and merge data only when it is necessary to do so. Double accounting is a waste of time and a misuse of system space. The reader may well be reading this and thinking, 'That's obvious – but how many people have names and addresses stored in a mail merge file as well as in a database? The probability is that this too is double accounting, for the data in the database store can be used as the source for mail merge.

Under-utilisation of RDBMS in HRM

Having argued that only applicable data should be stored within a system, it may seem strange that I have headed this section in such a way. However, I am of the opinion that HRM appears to be some way behind other users of computer-based management systems within organisations. A brief outline of the possible reasons was given in Chapter 1, not least of which was the reluctance to reduce individuals to a set of measurements, Data Protection legislation, and the possible inappropriateness of expert systems.

As a species we are at the top of the animal hierarchy in terms of our ability to think and to hypothesise. These and our many other cognitive abilities allow us to view things in rather more than stark yes or no decisions: we believe that we have to see things in various shades of grey. There are few absolute certainties in life, and few within the workplace, as far as human beings are concerned. One could argue that the whole of management science is based on the balancing of imponderables in a way that is acceptable to the situation and the individuals within the situation at that time and in that place. In relation to the current level of computer technology in common use, such philosophies are diametrically opposed to the way in which most systems make decisions based on binary yes or no options. This necessity to reduce situations to yes or no choices is probably instrumental in the scarce utilisation of computing within HRM decision-making. Even without considering the use of computer-aided decision-making, there is controversy within the field of HRM itself about whether individuals should be assessed against pre-defined criteria as a measure of performance, promotability, developability, etc. There can be no single answer to these debates: it depends on the philosophy of the individual organisation. For the purpose of this book we will assume that measuring the human resource against standards or requirements is acceptable. With this in mind we can then discuss the ways that a RDBMS can assist the management decision-making processes of HRM. I have already made it clear that I see computer technology as an aid to decision-making and to saving management time, not as a decision-maker in its own right. Automatically generated responses as a result of input data that cannot be countermanded must be avoided.

Having discussed the dangers and pitfalls of reducing people to a set of statistics or values, it could be argued that this is in fact how we make decisions about people in reality. It is just that as human beings we have the ability to question the validity of a value, and we are able to introduce a high number of factors and parameters into our decision-making process. I do not wish to alarm the reader – but so can computers. They have no problems with emotions and they do not get hangovers, but these aspects apart they can take into account the same sorts of variables as a human can in decision-making. They can also check values within a range of predetermined parameters. Of course they need to be told these things in advance, for the most part, and that is where they differ from us. We are able to introduce parameters and factors at will, sometimes at whim. What we in HRM seem to find difficult is defining requirements and parameters up-front. With a little thought it is possible to define parameters that can identify most of the requirements of a situation and allow us to utilise the search and sort capabilities of a computer to save us hours of work in manual searching. One benefit of using a computer in this way is that it will consider every file or record that it is asked to with the same effort and reliability. It does not get tired, it does not get distracted by phone-calls, and it does not try to second-guess the system and decide not to look in a particular place based on an instinctive feeling of low probability of success. If we can define our requirements well in the first place, therefore, the computer can give us a high-quality list of records that fit the requirement.

Chapter 4 uses just this approach to identify applicants who meet the specific requirements of a job. The system discards those that fail to meet the minimum requirement for the job and presents the details of those who match or exceed the requirement. Is there anything wrong with this approach?

Has anyone been treated unfairly? No, they have not – but what has been eliminated is the ability of the recruiting manager to use his or her instincts about the applicants.

Chapter 4 discusses recruitment further; sufficient to say at this point that it is the purpose of HRM to find the resource that can fulfil the requirements of the job and will enhance the organisation. The first of these conditions can be usefully enhanced by the computer; the second probably needs the skills of the human being to make professionally-based evaluations. By using the RDBMS to assist with the first part, management energy and time can be concentrated on the latter stage. Many people would put forward an emotive argument regarding the duty to read each applicant's details. This is inefficient in terms of resource utilisation and can bring HRM in for criticism from other sectors of organisations together with accusations of being a non-line function.

Clearly, many of the arguments and points above can be extended to aspects of HRM other than recruitment. Later chapters will look at managing appraisal systems and career development. To undertake this it will also be necessary to define measures that a system can make sense of. Performance review or appraisal usually includes some evaluation of performance that is categorised. Some may use the labels A, B, C, D, and E, although it could be argued that the inference that our society makes from these might make it better to use values from the middle of the alphabet like H, I, J, K, and L. From the computer's point of view it is easiest if the values are in alphabetical or chronological order: this allows ranking and grouping in reports to be undertaken easily by the system.

The key to using such ratings is the definition that accompanies them, but given a five-point scale it would make sense from the point of view of statistical analysis that the central value was the value that indicated that a person had achieved all of the objectives that had been agreed at the beginning of the measurement period. This is what they were being held accountable for, in the terms used in the philosophy of management by objectives.[1] This then leaves two measures on each side for under- or overperformers. These definitions also need to be couched in specific terms. Such a categorisation, as far as is possible, allows appraising managers to give honest

ratings. No system can cope with managers who are not prepared to be honest or who give easy objectives. This will be
discussed further in a later chapter.

The point to be made here is that at the end of the day
most of our people decisions are based on binary inputs. We
decompose all of the parameters of a decision until we
finally come down to a choice of yes or no. This really is not
very different from what happens in a computerised system.
However, this book is advocating that the machine should
aid and enhance decision-making for the HRM department,
not itself make the final decision. We have some way to go
in terms of technology and comfort levels before we are
ready to let the computer make the final decision without
interference from us.

Data Protection legislation forces us to make sure that the
information entered into a system is accurate. Without that
accuracy the data is useless anyway; we therefore need to
build in as many safeguards as possible. The computer can do
this more readily and easier than we human beings can. It is
very easy for a system to check against previous entries and
flag up a difference larger than might be expected. For exam
ple: in a system that manages a performance measurement
scheme an operator can be asked to confirm the input of a performance rating. This would probably only take a second, and
any mismatch between the two entries could be challenged
and the correct entry determined. Similarly, the system could
almost instantaneously check the current period input with
the previous period input and flag up where there is a differ
ential of two or more performance ratings. In my view data
input checks such as this make the data held in the system
more reliable and more usable than data stored in manual systems that is not verified in such ways.

It is to be hoped that this brief introduction to the ways that
data can be categorised, logged, checked and verified will help
the reader first to accept the potential robustness of data held
within a RDBMS, and furthermore to note that the data can
be used as an effective aid to management decision-making
and HRM system management.

Developing an application

The key to successful application development lies in the planning of the application and the key to successful maintenance and adaptation of new needs for an application lies in the documentation of the application at the development stage. Early software developers seldom documented any of the code that they wrote in order to achieve the system requirements.

A common term for early work like this was 'spaghetti code': the nature of the programming language was such that programs ran from start to finish in a linear fashion, looping off into subroutines and back to the main program. This made it very difficult to follow a program, and even more difficult to debug after it had been written. Real problems came when an application needed to be maintained or upgraded. Often the original programmer had moved jobs or projects, and there was no documentation to support the application. It was a case of a new programmer's having to try to analyse the code and to patch in new code to upgrade the system. An example of this – and one that may have far-reaching effects – is the date programming of the turn of the millennium at the year 2000. Many early programs were written using only two digits for the year number to save precious memory. Calculations on these are fine until the year 00 is reached. Adding 00 to 99 mathematically totals 99, but in actual time we know that it is going to be somewhere between 1 day and 365 days (it is understood that the year 2000 is not going to be a leap year) extra. For certain the banking sector will not give a year's free interest to everyone it deals with. The point is, however, that the software developers should have spotted this potential problem and built in an ability to cope.

Modern programming uses methods which allow software to be upgraded in small chunks or objects, without affecting the rest of the software. They are usually documented graphically, and can thus be maintained by people other than the original programmers.

While it is not advocated that HRM specialists become software engineers in order to develop applications, there are nevertheless some lessons that need to be learned even when developing the simple applications that this book deals with,

or when developing a spreadsheet application. It is amazing
how quickly we may forget how we managed to get a formula
in a spreadsheet to do a particular task. Utilising some simple
techniques at the outset can save a great deal of time later on.
In the case of a spreadsheet, notes can be entered onto the
sheet and hidden from normal view; formulae can refer to
named ranges, such as 'current salary' rather than a cell
address; and lastly, effective spreadsheet packages such as
Excel have diagnostic tools incorporated which allow the
sheet to audit itself. These are not foolproof, but they can certainly help trace an error.

As for developing applications that run in a RDBMS, the
documentation needs to be a little more comprehensive. At
the very least a statement of outcomes must be written, stating exactly what it is the system will do when it is completed.
Such statements must include range parameters as well. That
is the system will

- store all periods of absence from work by employee
- identify the reason for absence against a predefined table of
  possibilities
- report the number of workdays absent for each occurrence
  and in total by employee
- report all absences by reason code and accounting period,
  by department and location
- report the cost to the organisation of all absences other
  than legitimate holidays taken
- report all proposed holidays to be taken, but not yet taken,
  by employee, department and location.

Having identified what it is that the developer seeks to
achieve, we can start thinking about the new data that needs
to be stored. Remember: much of the data will be stored in
tables that may well already exist. A table with personal
employee details will certainly exist, and for the purposes of
this example let us say that job details, location and department are held elsewhere in the system, as are salary details.
For this application, additional data that will be required is
therefore absence occurrences and absence classifications.

Table 9
ATTENDANCE TABLE

FIELD NAME	FIELD TYPE	COMMENT
EMPLOYEE NUMBER	NUMERICAL	LINK FIELD TO EMPLOYEE DETAILS
ABSENCE DATE	DATE FIELD	
RETURN DATE	DATE FIELD	REPORTS CALCULATE WORKING DAYS ABSENT
REASON CODE	ALPHA NUMERIC	LINKS REASON CODE TABLE , MUST ONLY ACCEPT IDENTIFIED CODES

Table 10
ATTENDANCE REASON CODE TABLE

REASON CODE	FULL TEXT OF REASON CODE
A	AUTHORISED ABSENCE
H	HOLIDAY TAKEN
LU	UNPAID LEAVE
PH	PROPOSED HOLIDAY
S	SICKNESS
U	UNAUTHORISED ABSENCE

The developer will need to select the names of the proposed data tables and the data fields to be placed in them in the same way as that used in Chapter 2. Additionally, the developer will need to identify the type of data field that is intended, in order to make calculations and indexing easier for the database. Tables 9 and 10 show the data fields that could be used.

In Table 9 there is sufficient data for the computer to calculate the number of working days off. True, the operator could enter the number of days – but that is open to error, whereas once the computer knows the normal working days of the person and any bank holidays, it can be quickly and accurately calculated.

In a previous chapter we discussed the need for input to be consistent if the data was to produce reliable information. Table 10 shows one way in which this can be achieved. By presenting another table with the possible absence reason codes and their explanations, it is possible for the program to allow the input person to select from this list when entering a code in the absence details table. On selecting the reason from a drop-down box, the reason code will automatically be inserted into the field in the attendance details table. The system will not allow any non-acceptable code to be entered.. Illegal data will not permit a valid analysis of the input data. By planning the requirements of the application and the inputs needed to achieve it, therefore, the application will operate to specification more quickly. The documentation makes the system auditable, testable and modifiable without too much relearning and reworking.

Within the documentation and development it is also crucial to utilise some form of system configuration. This means that at each stage or each trial or each re-specification it is crucial that there is some method of identifying the latest documentation version. There are a number of ways in which this can be done. Each document can be given a number which identifies it. Every time a document is saved or printed, most word processors allow a field to be inserted into the header or footer section that logs and increments the date and time of saving or printing. By using such techniques within the development documentation, a developer can always be sure that he or she is working on the latest version. Likewise when developing the actual application, that can be saved with a version number included in the save details.

Development configuration is not a topic that switches a lot of people on, but nevertheless, with just a little effort at the outset a great deal of time can be saved later. The payback can far outweigh the investment. Any reader who is considering developing a relatively complex application must be prepared to adopt configuration management techniques. Further reading on the subject than has been briefly outlined here is essential. A relatively easy book to use as an introduction to the topic has been written by Britton and Doake.[2]

Prototyping and developing an application

Any application other than the simplest of spreadsheets will probably be best developed by using the technique known as prototyping. Prototyping is the method of developing an application a bit at a time, either in sections that are then added together to make the whole application or by incrementally building the application. Whichever of these methods is used, it is important to rigorously test whatever has been developed at each stage, thus ensuring that at each section or increment it can be shown that the application does what is expected at that point – so that if any unexpected occurrences happen later on it will be possible to be confident that the early stages of application development are robust.

Testing of the sections should be rigorous. The purpose of the testing is twofold: a) to establish that the application works as predicted; and b) to establish that the application does not fail when information entered is outside the acceptable parameters.

For example: if a routine called for the entry of a person's date of birth, the system needs to be tested to check that

- the input is translated as a date
- the right date of birth is entered
- that it is in an acceptable and consistent date format
- date formats are aligned to the conventions of the country in which the system will operate
- dates outside an age range of 16 to 65 are highlighted and rejected, and re-entry is called for
- dates entered incorrectly are corrected
- dates incorrectly entered for dates forward of the current day's date are rejected and do not crash the system
- nothing untoward will happen to two-digit year entries after a change of century
- nothing untoward will happen to four-digit year entries.

This list covers most of the aspects for testing a date of birth entry. It is much better to discover an unexpected outcome as the application is developed rather than to have to try to debug a whole application after it has supposedly been completed.

Testing should include a sample of likely entries within the acceptable range and a sample of entries that fall outside the acceptable range but are nevertheless possible inputs to the system. It can never be guaranteed that an application is bug-free – but if the bugs do not surface, they are not important to find.

In the prototyping, attention should be paid to the interface between the user and the computer. Too often too little attention is given to this aspect, and the system is not as easy and straightforward to use as it could have been with a little thought.

One of the most frustrating aspects of input from an input document can occur when the system asks for data to be input in an order or format different from the input document. This is relatively simple to overcome at the time of application design by ensuring that the input screen form is in the same order or format as the hard-copy document, or vice versa. It is not so easy to correct after the screen form has been developed. In some RDBMS host shells, the cursor moves from data field to data field in the order that the fields were originally placed on the sheet – so the cursor may not automatically move to the next field in a sequential order when the enter key is pressed on the field that is visually in front of the amended data field. Likewise a field that is moved on the screen form may well still cause the cursor to pass on to it in the same order as the original location of the field.

With a little thought in advance, such problems can be avoided. By thinking about the hard-copy input document in advance, the screen form can be made to mirror this input document. From the input person's point of view it is much easier to input data in the same format and sequence as the source document.

Much of the interface between machine and user is determined by the operating system anyway. For example: if the application that you are developing is running on Access or Paradox or similar, then the interface will be running within the Microsoft Windows environment and the major features of the screen will be predetermined. The user will be able to add items to the drop-down menus and delete some others, but in general the features of the interface will be dictated. What is available for the application developer to determine is the design of the individual windows that will be used as input or output screens. These screens should be carefully and logically laid out, with little clutter and, perhaps most importantly, big enough font sizes for the user to read and without a blaze of different colours. Prototyping can help significantly in the development of these screens. Dummy screens can even be developed on a different package: Powerpoint or Excel, for instance, can be used for developing prototype screens to test against the person who will input the data.

Generally, for backgrounds neutral or pastel colours are best. These are more restful to the eyes and also allow the eyes to concentrate on the text (which is where the information is contained). Do not use more than three colours on the screen – apart from short-stay messages which flag up errors or which contain information to make choices from (such as a drop-down box that is clicked on to determine the next move or entry).

Colours that can be used as background combinations without being distracting or uncomfortable are grey, dark blue, gold, mid-green and magenta. Using bright reds and greens in combination can cause the eye to flick from one to the other, and may well result in discomfort and eyestrain over time. Look at the screen colours of most commercially available packages and you will see that few, if any, use bright screen colours for anything other than warning messages. One of the most-used combinations is white or yellow text on a blue background. Experiment by prototyping to find the most effective screen colour combination for your purpose.

One further area to consider with screen development is consistency. It is useful from a user's point of view if all input screens have a similar colour scheme and layout, and if output or report screens have a different but equally consistent style. Screens should be clearly labelled regarding their function or purpose. In this way the application starts to become more user-friendly.

System security

In Chapter 1 an outline of the Data Protection legislation identified how important it is for employee data to be secure. This may be seen as an arduous imposition, but surely none of us would want our personal details available to anyone who had the ability to interrogate a database. As we have seen from previous chapters, the links that can be made between various tables in a RDBMS can lead to some very detailed information's being gathered relatively easily. Even a manual system using filing cabinets can be locked – and, what is more, it is less available to linked interrogation. It is therefore reasonable that safeguards should be built into the system that allow security of access to data.

Any application that is developed, whether on a spreadsheet, database, or even a word processor, can be password-protected to avoid unwanted access.

Securing the whole file

The simplest form of security is to password-protect the whole file. This is normal when used in conjunction with a word-processed file. In MS Word a file can be easily protected in one of two ways by selecting the 'Options' button from the 'Save as dialogue' box. Selecting this option gives access to another dialogue box which allows the user to prevent other people from opening a file without a password, thereby denying access at all. Alternatively, the file can be saved with a write-reservation password attached. This is useful if, for instance, the staff handbook or terms and conditions documents are saved as proforma documents. To secure a document as a write reservation document means that the current user cannot make any permanent changes to the document, for the system will not allow the document to be saved back under the same name, thus preserving the original document.

The developer or file owner may of course want to protect a whole file that is a spreadsheet or a RDBMS file. A similar process will have to be gone through which prevents the opening of the file. Note that once a file has been protected, it can be opened only by using the password. Many host software applications, such as Access 2, encrypt or scramble the data when it is protected. Once this is done, nobody can unscramble it. Even if the manufacturer of the host software could help, they would not. SO DO NOT FORGET THE PASSWORDS THAT HAVE BEEN ASSIGNED!

Different levels of application protection

With spreadsheet protection and RDBMS applications it may

also be desirable to protect different sections of an application from different levels of user. The process of protection for the two types of application are quite different, and are accordingly dealt with separately.

Spreadsheet protection

Protecting a spreadsheet can be achieved in a number of ways. In the case of Excel and other three-dimensional spreadsheets, if the whole file is protected by a password then access cannot be gained to any part of the file or workbook. This is all right if this is truly the intention – but it is more normally a requirement that an application can be opened by a user other than the developer, and that data can be entered to achieve some previously formulated information output. By utilising the power of the three-dimensional nature of modern spreadsheet packages it is possible, even desirable, to have all of the formulae entered on a different data sheet, hide this from the user, and password-protect it as well. In this way the user cannot alter any of the calculated cells. The workbook can also be write-protected. This prevents a file of the same name from being saved, so that the original file is always loaded. The workbook can be saved under a new name – which is useful if the file is designed to produce a monthly report from an original file that contains the formulated cell relationships and requires the data to be entered each month for analysis. The workbook can otherwise be saved by month name, leaving the original unaltered.

It may not be feasible to give unrestricted access to every workbook. Within a data sheet individual cells can be locked so that no physical change can be made to the data contained in them: a locked cell containing a formula will change its value according to the input data – the whole cell with its formula can show a different value, but the formula itself cannot be changed.

The spreadsheet will have a facility to lock the sheet. In Excel 5 this can be found in the tools menu. However, this locks every cell in the sheet by default. Any cell into which a user wishes still to be able to enter data will have to be unlocked. This can be achieved via the format cells option and must be done before locking the sheet. If the designer wants a user to be able to enter data but not to alter formulae, therefore, it will be necessary to create a facility to unlock the cells where data is to be entered and then protect the spread-sheet. This will allow data entry in the nominated unlocked cells. It is also a good idea to choose the option that hides for-mulae as well: this can be effected while locking or unlocking cells.

Locking, protecting and hiding are the three main ways of ensuring that a workbook cannot be accidentally corrupted by a user. A combination of these techniques can bring about a comprehensive security system but will not make the system foolproof: files should be backed up in the event of accidental deletion by the user. The workbook can be made to save a back-up copy each time it is saved, if it is not a read-only file.

RDBMS protection

The nature and sensitivity of the data held in a RDBMS mean that the security system attached to it has to be more com-prehensive. In addition there have to be different levels of interactivity in the system as required by different people. Some users will need only to be able to get access to certain reports, while others will need input access only, without any ability to delete entries or records or to produce reports. It will also be necessary for the developer, at least, to have total access to the application. By default, host database shells give complete access to all of the tables, reports, queries, forms, macros, etc that have been developed. This situation should be left as it is until an application has been written and tested.

Once the developer is happy with the application, a listing of levels of authority can be made. Principally, there are three levels: administrator, system users and guests. These levels dictate the type of use a person can have. Each individual can additionally have certain tables or functions made available to him or her and be excluded from others. For example, an input clerk in one department should not be able to gain access to the input information for any other department. When start-ing to restrict access to the system, the first thing that a devel-oper must do is to ensure that he or she has total access to all features of the application. This must be done before the default total access authority is removed, as that authority must be if any security is to be maintained. If developers do not introduce a coded total access for themselves, they can easily exclude themselves from the system. In many systems, once this has been done access cannot be reinstated. It is a good idea to keep an archived back-up of the application unprotected but without sensitive data. At least by doing this the application can be reinstated and data can be reloaded if it is available. Imagine reloading all of the data into a HRIS: it probably would not be feasible.

Individual host RDBMS have different ways of authorising different user's access to the system. A developer needs to think most carefully about who should have access, and to what degree. It is even more of a problem when using a net-worked system that is having its data entered from remote sites. One old argument suggests that all reports should be generated by request, by HRM. This is a severe limitation on the usability of the system. Sometimes, however, it may be the only way to ensure security of data.

It is not the intention here to go into an extended explana-tion of system security because each application will have dif-ferent techniques for achieving it. At the very least developers should think about access to individual tables and reports, and whether users should be given permission to delete entries or whether that should be allowed only to a system administrator. Indeed, correctly entered, records should never be deleted because that could seriously jeopardise the validity of the data. For example: if a personal details record were to be deleted, all of its associated data would be homeless and might not be available for statistical analysis or auditing. Although legislation prevents us from keeping personally iden-tifiable details for longer than is necessary, it is possible to purge a name and address from the system but still keep all the details that we need for analysis such as gender, etc.

Data security is a potential minefield – but with careful planning and thought it is possible to ensure, as far as is rea-sonably practicable, that data is secure.

The data needs to be secure while being used and while not in use. Back-ups should be taken at intervals that the user defines as being the period of time for which it is practical and possible to re-enter lost data. In most cases it should be on a daily basis. With sensitive and important data it is advisable to take more than one back-up copy and to store one of them off-site. It is a good idea to have a back-up disk or tape for each day of the week and to rotate them. This means that in the event of a disaster on-site, relatively up-to-date information can be generated. The disks or tapes should also be periodically audited to ensure that they will in fact run the application. There is little point in archiving data that will not support the application.

Electronically stored data is volatile and can easily be corrupted: it is worth mentioning a few common pitfalls that relate to such storage. Any magnetic source can corrupt data. These include telephones – particularly a handset – loudspeakers in appliances (for example, Dictaphones in the same briefcase as the data disk), and some catches on handbags and briefcases are magnetic. Microwave sources can also corrupt data. There is one reported case of a person taking a diskette with him to the microwave while he heated his lunch. The disk was placed on top of the oven, which had a slight radiation leak. This was enough to corrupt the data on the disk.

Despite all of the sophisticated ways to protect data that can be incorporated within an application and the pitfalls of external corruption, it is my personal experience that there is a potentially greater peril at large than all of those so far mentioned: the operator. How many times have you, the reader, walked through a deserted office only to see a computer left switched on and an application running? Many systems have a time-out mechanism which exits the logged-on user from the system if no entry is made for a pre-defined period of time. Nevertheless, it is still possible to get into the data before the time-out.

If the user is logged-on, anyone who then uses the machine will have the same access rights as the logged-on user. Only discipline can overcome this potential hazard.

This chapter has shown the importance of deciding what to store and how to store it. It has also discussed the need for controlling, planning, preparing, prototyping and testing an application as it develops. The chapter concludes by looking at ways of making data secure, the importance of which cannot be overstressed. Through the techniques outlined in this chapter, applications can be made more robust, easier to use by other people, maintainable and auditable. If an original application fits these requirements, it can be continuously enhanced and developed with more up-to-date versions that fit the needs of the developing business.

References

1   DRUCKER, P. 'The practice of management' in L. Mullins (ed.), *Management and Organisational Behaviour*, 4th edn, London, Pitman, 1996, p. 447.
2   BRITTON, C. *and* DOAKE J. *Software Systems Development: A gentle introduction.* London, McGraw-Hill International, 1993.

4

RECRUITMENT AND SELECTION

Recruitment and selection is one of the areas to which a computerised database can offer much to help in controlling the process and reducing the amount of managerial time spent on the activity.

The process of recruitment can be viewed as a linear process, and as such readily lends itself to the algorithmic approach of computer software. An algorithm of a possible recruitment process is illustrated in Figure 4 which should not be seen as an idealised model of the recruitment process but rather as a working outline for the purposes of this chapter. However, it is a perfectly feasible process illustration for the recruitment of staff. In some cases not all of the processes would need to be undertaken.

Process control

The level of control that an HRM department might have in the recruitment process doubtless varies from organisation to organisation and indeed from vacancy to vacancy. It is perfectly feasible, in these days of devolving responsibility to functional and operational managers, that many of the lower-level jobs in an organisation may be recruited by departmental managers without any physical involvement from HRM. At the middle to higher levels of organisational responsibility, meanwhile, where the risks to the business of making a recruitment mistake are high, the level of HRM involvement may be significantly greater. Nevertheless, in most organisations it will be seen as part of the responsibility of HRM either to define the organisational shape and headcount, in

Figure 4
THE RECRUITMENT ALGORITHM

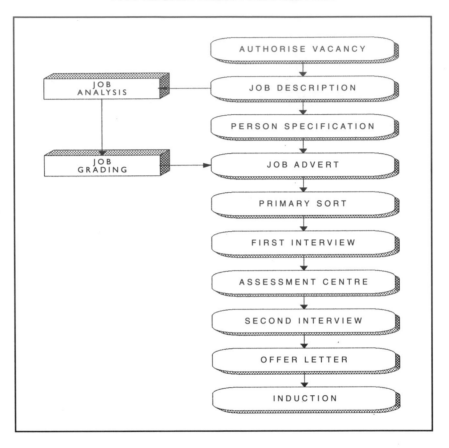

conjunction with the line managers, or to monitor an agreed headcount.

It is therefore possible to develop a relatively simple database application, using off-the-shelf software such as Paradox or Microsoft Access Relational Database Management Systems. The sophistication-level requirement of the eventual application will depend on the needs of the user. The application could be little more than a series of data tables and queries that can be used to trigger letters and reports. Such an application would probably need a person with a good knowledge of the RDBMS host shell for this approach to be successful.

Alternatively, and most probably, it could be a standalone application that guides the user through the various stages using predefined forms to aid input. A successful software application would also control the process and prevent unauthorised recruitment taking place.

The remainder of this chapter examines each of the identified stages in some detail, looking at ways in which current low-cost PC-based software could be used to enhance the recruitment process.

Instigation and authorisation of a vacancy

There can be very few organisations that do not practise some form of headcount control. The obvious place to start looking at controlling the headcount is the stage at which a vacancy is initially identified. In an organisation that is practising resource planning alongside its production forecasting processes, the forecast recruitment for expansion will be a regulated process that ties in recruitment with phased business expansion.

For example: if a sales organisation has forecast an x per cent increase in sales during the coming year in new markets, it may well forecast the requirement to take on a new sales staff member in month 7 of the business year. The use of a predefined computerised spreadsheet such as Lotus 123 or Microsoft Excel could assist the person responsible for the recruitment budget to build a phased budget which not only helps to control the cost but also helps to control the process by flagging up the time to run a planned recruitment campaign.

By undertaking the process of planning, job evaluation, forecasting and budgeting of the recruitment process well in advance, the issue of what the job is likely to cost the organisation can be dealt with and a realistic salary figure entered. At the time of recruitment this will be used as a control. Without such a process it is possible that a salary higher than necessary might be paid to a person who happened to be popular at interview.

The computer can add a process that will enhance the recruitment method. At this vacancy authorisation stage, it is control data that will be fed into the computer rather than information that will come out of the computer. Nevertheless, this process can cause organisations to think about the whole process of recruitment-initiating procedures which can ensure that systems cannot be circumvented. The suggested inputs in this section presuppose that the department that is to undertake the recruitment also has control of the advertising, whether as an accountability for managing the process or as an accountability for the budget. This is not intended as a mechanism by which an HRM department may wield power over the organisation, but more to ensure that agreed policies and procedures are utilised to gain maximum advantage for the organisation. Many organisations insist, for instance, that all advertising is placed with an agreed format and logo. One way to achieve this is to focus the effort as the responsibility of one person.

It cannot be denied that in order to reap the benefits that a RDBMS can bring to the recruitment process there will of necessity be an amount of time to be spent inputting data once the system has been set up. This is true of any control or quality assurance system, whether manual or computer-driven. It can be argued that the benefits to the organisation are outweighed by the cost of undertaking the process. It is my personal view that it depends on the type of data input into the system and the use made of the data once it has been entered. It is true that in initiating any system there has to be a desire to improve a process on the part of the user, whether that improvement is in quality of outcome or in efficiency of the process, or in both. The suggestions that are made for the use of a computer in the recruitment process can enhance the control system, reduce the amount of management time spent on the process, and assist in identifying and achieving the selection of a suitable candidate with the required job skills.

The data required for registering a vacancy in any organisation will probably be gathered and stored manually in an existing system. All that is required at this stage is for this datasheet to be viewed as an input document to a system which is held locally on a PC. The recruitment management application could be networked to allow access by many, but it does not need to be linked to the HR record-keeping database; it should rather be a standalone system.

The data fields required to initiate recruitment application will vary from organisation to organisation. The following suggestions can be seen as a generic start point.

Vacancy details table

In keeping with the recommended techniques for developing a RDBMS, small linked tables should be built up which allow a user to cross-reference data at a later stage and also to develop the data as recruitment progresses.

At this point we need to think about the fundamental data items relating to a vacancy that will be unique to this stage of the recruitment.

A representative data table name should be chosen: here 'Vacancy details' will be used. The syntax of the table name will vary according to the host database shell in use. Some allow blank spaces, some do not; others limit the number of characters.

The details that are unique to this stage of the recruitment process and are representative of the vacancy authorisation process should be added as data fields to this table. The following sections represent a suggested list.

Vacancy number

This must be a unique number which identifies one particular vacancy. Most database shells can do this automatically by nominating the data type for the field as a counter. There will also be a facility to ensure that this number cannot be repeated in this table, which will ensure that any reference to this vacancy number from another data table will always link back to this (and only this) data record. In the event of a user's trying to key in the number again as an input for a different vacancy record, the system will commence a prevention routine.

This feature is fundamental to database management and helps maintain data integrity. It would be absolutely no use to anyone if we could not be sure that the system was always referring back to the same data records for its data analysis.

Furthermore, most database shells do not allow the deletion of a key data field with this counter number. In practice this means that the data record number will never be reusable, even if the associated data has been purged from the system.

Date field

Why put in a date field? At some future time you may wish to set targets for filling vacancies or analyse the average time taken to fill vacancies. Without the initiation date in the table, that would not be a possibility. Date fields can be entered into many of the tables that are seen as necessary to manage the process. By doing this, a time analysis of each step can be undertaken, if so desired. This may seem an arduous task, but as with most reports from a database, a regularly required report needs to be set up only once: it can then be run on request, without having to set up the requirement again.

Entering dates into a system can usually be achieved very easily. The data field can be set up to enter today's date by default, with the ability to overtype with any other date that is required. Since in most cases it is today's date that should be entered, it is simply a requirement to press 'Enter' at the field.

Job details

A number of data fields are required here to identify the job. For example: job title, department, location, replacement or new job, date required by, and job type.

The important thing is consistency of input. Current levels of database technology mean that searching for data matches is performed on the basis of character recognition and not on the underlying semantic meaning of words. Whereas a human will probably interpret B'ham and Birmingham to mean the same thing in the context of a job location, the computer would not. This is not the problem it might appear to be. These data fields can be set up to accept only certain inputs (whole words or abbreviations), thus ensuring consistency. Even better, with many database host shells – particularly Windows™ and Apple Macintosh™ systems – it is possible to set up a list box which allows the user to choose an entry from a list. This ensures a valid entry.

In the case of the data fields in question, it is likely that department, location and job type fields identified would need list box entries. The job title is less likely to need such a list, and new or replacement job would be a one-letter entry of 'N' or 'R'.

The data field descriptions are self-explanatory, perhaps with the exception of the job type. A useful analysis tool at a later stage is an ability to classify jobs by type rather than by title. Job titles in a department may vary, but the jobs may be basically quite similar. For instance, a wage clerk and a payroll assistant would not be grouped together by their job title according to a computer search. However, if they were identified as payroll in the department field and as clerical in the job type field, a grouping search on these two fields would list them together, thus yielding meaningful information. Classifications for the job type field might include executive, manager, supervisor, clerical, operative, manual and research, among others.

All of these can be put into the default list. To save computer memory, the actual entry in the database can be an abbreviated code for each identified variant, which is then reconverted at report printout stage.

Putting in coded entries in a database is commonly used as a way of both saving memory (as mentioned) and reducing input time.

Budget details

There are two major areas to enquire about at this stage. Is the job salary budgeted for? Is the recruitment budgeted for? Simple 'Y' or 'N' data fields will give the information required. It may additionally be desirable to include a field for a proposed salary, although this is not essential. A link could also be made to other data tables that hold the salary details, which could be linked via the proposed grade of the job.

There is more advantage to the user to add extra data about the recruitment process. Is the recruitment to be managed internally or by an agency? Is the job to be advertised? Although these data fields can be completed with a simple yes or no, they can be considered as key to the control of the recruitment process.

Given that the system already holds details about the job

type, location, department, etc, and will eventually hold details about the job grade or level of job, it is possible to introduce some controls into the process, if so desired.

If the actual salary range for a level or grade was above or below the requested salary, this would be highlighted by the system and would need to be resolved before the process could continue. Wage drift as a result of poor control would be prevented. Such a report would be automatically generated by the system, and further entries to the process or actions by the system could be barred until the problem was resolved.

The recruitment budget could be controlled on the basis of maximum permissible expenditure for different levels, types or locations of jobs. A separate data table could be set up that identified type of job, whether agencies might be used, whether advertisements might be placed, and the maximum advertising cost. The data combination of entries in the job details table could be compared with those in the budget table. Where a mismatch occurred, the process would need to be reconciled before the system allowed the process to continue. A mismatch is most likely to happen at the stage of placing advertising. At this time the quoted cost of the advert could be inserted into the system and matched. If it was a mismatch, the advert would have to be redrafted to ensure that it came within budget.

Authorisation

Finally, details of the initiating manager and the authorising manager need to be logged in the vacancy details table. These comprise no more than two data fields: one for each surname and one for each forename, although they will of course require distinct data field names. Another approach to this could be to use the employee's number for identification purposes. This could be achieved by using the drop-down box approach, picking the employee's name from a list and clicking on it so that the database shell inserts the employee number in the data table.

There are a number of other points to bear in mind. How do you know that the John Smith or Sarah Jones is the one that you mean to put into the new data record? The best way around this is to include several data fields in the drop-down box. The employee's job title and location in addition to the name would probably be enough. If there is still confusion, you could check the employee number anyway.

You are probably thinking that it is a lot of effort to generate all of this information. That need not be the case. Although the system under discussion has been referred to as a standalone system, it does not mean that it cannot import data from another system. Most RDBMS shells store data in a way in which it can be queried and exported to a table, and can then be read by another database shell or different application using the same host. It is therefore just a question of exporting the name, job title, employee number and location of all authorised employees to a table, and referencing it in the recruitment control application.

You may also choose to add a data field that identifies authorisation levels. Once that is done, the system can be easily made to check the authority level of the person who initiates the request for a vacancy to be created and of the person who authorises recruitment to fill the vacancy.

Vacancy details summary

By creating the vacancy details table, you will have a collection of data fields that will include most, if not all, of the

Table 11
VACANCY DETAILS DATA TABLE

Vacancy identification number (unique)
Date of entry
Vacancy budgeted for?
Job title
Date required by
Department
Proposed salary
Location
Manage recruitment internally?
Replacement or New job
Use external agency?
Date required
Is advertising to be done?
Job type
Initiating manager details
Authorising manager details

fields in Table 11. The system only has to be set up once, and then it is just a question of inputting the data for each vacancy as it occurs. The input document is only a formalisation of what must happen already to control recruitment in an organisation.

The level of sophistication required by an organisation will probably depend on the size of the organisation or the way in which the organisation usually controls its activities. A great advantage of using a computerised process is that the input and administration of the system need not take up management time but is automatically controlled as if a manager were undertaking the tasks.

Even with this small number of data fields, reports can be produced that show the level of recruiting being implemented by department, by job type, by location, and by manager. Exception reports can flag up anomalies to the agreed parameters.

If an organisation has a turnover problem, reports of the above nature can be valuable in discovering possible causes of the high turnover.

System output reports are covered in a later section.

What can a computer add?

As with all recruitment campaigns, a major key to success is the ability of the organisation to identify the absolute standard that is required as a minimum for the job. It is no easy task to achieve this – indeed, many managers would say that it is not necessary. 'I know what I'm looking for' or 'I can pick 'em' are phrases often heard when asking a manager what it is that is required of a potential employee.

The problem with this approach is that the classic 'halo-or-horns' effect can occur.

A computer cannot determine whether or not a manager will like a person – but I personally believe that that is probably one of the most important factors towards eventual success in a job. A person is unlikely to be successful in a job if the boss does not like him or her. What is required is to make sure that only people who have the skills predicted for job success get through to the final decision stage, so that personality factors may exert an influence for or against only candidates who are known to be suitable otherwise.

It is also my firm view that at the end of a recruitment campaign it is seldom, if ever, possible to say categorically that 'We have recruited the best person.' That is a statement that is difficult to prove. What an organisation really needs to be able to say is that 'We have recruited a person who we know has the knowledge, skills and experience identified as a prerequisite, and who we believe will fit in well with the company culture and has the ambition to grow in the job.'

An ongoing controversy holds that people cannot be reduced to a series of numerical values or yes and no decisions. This philosophy is probably the reason computers do not seem to have infiltrated the management decision-making process of human resource management in the same way that they have in modelling finance decisions or production decisions. Although the philosophy must in part be true, when making a final decision in the recruiting process surely it must ultimately be down to a stark yes or no decision? It is the effectiveness of the evidence-gathering process that helps the final decision to be the right one.

Certainly not all questions regarding ability and performance can be preordained or built into a computer program. Indeed, interviewing is a key skill in the recruitment process. It is as important to see how a candidate formulates an answer as it is to listen to the answer. Nevertheless, there must be a set of perhaps six absolute minimum criteria for a position, and any candidate who does not come up to them cannot be considered for interview. It is in this area that the computer can assist a recruiting manager and save many hours' reading non-job-specific application forms or a multitude of CVs, all of which are laid out differently and designed to sell the person's strengths and hide his or her weaknesses.

The computer should be viewed as an aid to decision-making rather than as the decision-maker for the final selection. In the suggested ways of using the computer it will be seen that a computer will not necessarily make any decisions but merely implement instructions.

The science of recruiting can be seen as a methodology designed to minimise the risk to an organisation when employing people to undertake its business or function. Computer analysis of data using predefined criteria is one way of making risk minimisation more effective.

Identifying key factors of the job

Recruitment best practice would hold that all jobs for which staff are being recruited must have been subject to some form of job analysis, so that there now exists a list of accountability areas and responsibilities together with a statement of the basic purpose or aim of each job. Even if the organisation does not go as far as having a formal job description, at least the required job outputs must have been identified.

Recent developments in the identification of standards of competence in managerial and supervisory jobs can assist the process of identifying what level of competence is required for any particular job.

In order to be able usefully and meaningfully to assess the ability of candidates to achieve the minimum requirements of a job, six minimum standards of ability need to be established. These minimum standards must be absolute, and therefore realistic. If a manager has said that a person needs to have 'A'-level maths, that *must* be the case. Many managers in the past have made minimum standard statements only to change them when a candidate they like falls short of the stated requirement. It cannot be stressed enough that *the minimum standard is the minimum need*.

It is here that the job competence standards that have been developed can be useful. If holding meetings is an essential feature of the job being recruited, the statement of competence in holding meetings at the appropriate job level could be used as the statement of minimum standard.

Personal characteristics can be identified if necessary, but attributes such as age are becoming increasingly less important in recruitment. Indeed, adopting selection criteria based solely on ability and experience should assist an organisation to steer clear of possible equal opportunity problems.

Applying the need to the computer

What is required at this stage, then, is for the computer

application to be able to allocate some space to entering the criteria, and then to be able to compare the applicant with them either manually or automatically.

In the section on the vacancy details table we looked at data fields. Most of the fields that we used in that table were either date, numeric or short word fields. In the table that we develop for the job criteria we will need to enter statements containing many words. In most RDBMS shells alpha-numeric fields can contain up to 256 characters. This will be enough, with careful definition of the requirement. By using an alpha-numeric field we can at any time search our database using key word searches. This will be useful as the database of competency statements builds up, because we may not need to start from scratch for each job criteria statement but borrow or adapt previous ones.

Job criteria table

The data fields that are suggested for this data table will link the minimum criteria to the job number and prioritise them. There are at least two ways in which this can be achieved.

Option 1

Earlier it was suggested that up to six criteria should be iden-tified for each job in order to measure whether a person met the minimum criteria for the vacancy. Logically, then, we might expect to have a data table that had the data fields shown in Table 12.

This takes up a lot of space on the page, and would take up even more space in a computer. One of the features of most

Table 12
JOB CRITERIA: OPTION 1

Job number   (Key field) links back to the vacancy details table.
Date
Criterion 1
Criterion 2
Criterion 3
Criterion 4
Criterion 5
Criterion 6

databases is that each field in a record has to have a nominated length. In the example shown, the job number field would probably be allocated ten digits, the date eight, and each of the criteria fields would be allocated 256 characters of space. With the table configured as displayed, the computer would reserve space in its memory for 1,554 characters as soon as the record was opened. It could also be the case that the user might want to change the order of priority of the criteria. Using the above technique would mean moving the data from one field to another. This would probably mean retyping the entries.

Option 2

A neater way to achieve exactly the same thing could be carried out as in Table 13. Each record in this example would only need about 280 characters of space reserved in the memory: a significant saving. Another advantage is that the priority of any criterion can be changed just by overtyping the priority value entry; equivalent rankings can be used, or the field can be left blank if there is no need to rank the criteria.

The only downside to this technique is the need to enter the job number for each criterion, but that is a small price to pay for the added benefits. Additionally, using Option 2 does not lead the system user to enter six criteria just because there is space. There will be many jobs that may not have six 'knockout' criteria. Option 2 is more user-friendly in this respect. Option 2 even allows *more* than six criteria if necessary; Option 1 does not.

For the purposes of this book, Option 2 will be used.

Examples of minimum requirement statements

Information for the criteria can be drawn from a number of

Table 13
OPTION 2 DATA FIELDS

Job number
Date
Job criteria
Priority value

places in the recruitment cycle: the job description, the person specification, job evaluation data, salary grade bands, and the potential manager of the position. The latter must have an input into the process and also be the person to sign off the criteria as being the minimum acceptable.

This is no more than would normally be done in an effective recruitment environment. The only extra work is the input of the criteria into a computer. Once defined, these can be typed in by anyone – it does not need management time.

The key question to ask the manager is, 'Would you accept an applicant that fell one order of magnitude short of your criterion?'

When the answer is an emphatic 'No' – that is the minimum standard.

Another way of finding the minimum criterion could be to ask, 'What would prevent a person from doing this job?' This is likely to raise such issues as physical restrictions – for example, an inability to lift 20-kilo sacks.

Undertaking this exercise also helps to prevent statements from being made that could be seen as contravening company policies or equal opportunities legislation.

A series of prioritised statements should be the result of the investigation. An applicant might therefore be required to have

1   a degree in mechanical engineering
2   managed a production environment manufacturing perishable products for at least two years
3   managed a production environment with responsibility for quality assurance, production and packaging for at least two years
4   directly supervised non-engineering and engineering personnel in a manufacturing process for a minimum of two years
5   not earned more than the current maximum salary on offer in the last employment.

It must be remembered that these are the minimum standards – but they will nevertheless weed out many of the applicants.

The criteria listed above have been prioritised and can be entered into the job criteria table.

The job advertisement

Budget control

The computerised recruitment application is not intended to be able to prepare job advertisements. It can nevertheless assist in controlling the budget for adverts in the way described earlier, by setting up maximum advertising budgets depending on the level of the vacancy being recruited and perhaps also on the location. It is a simple matter to set up a small data table that requires the vacancy number and the proposed cost of the advertisement. If this exceeds the amount identified in the control tables for this vacancy type and/or location, the system would flag it up to the user. The system could be set to prevent further action until the conflict is resolved or some password that allows the budget overspend to be authorised by a manager. This may seem to the reader to be unnecessary, and indeed it may well be. It depends on who is running the system – but since the objective is to allow the system to be run by non-managerial staff it may well be worth spending the time to build in such safeguards.

Advert content

Although the computerised database system has little to offer this stage of the process, other computer packages certainly have much more.

Desktop publishing or even simple graphics packages can enable organisations to undertake the artwork for an advertisement, thereby substantially reducing the cost of advertising. A major benefit of this is that it is possible with most packages to construct a template that becomes a standard layout for all company adverts. A quick glance through any recruitment section of a newspaper reveals that many organisations adopt this approach. Moreover, if a company logo is used in a standard layout, potential employees may be drawn to the advertisement by implicitly recognising the brand.

Once a design has been produced and agreed, it can be stored as a template and its size adapted for each vacancy. Again it can be seen that a small amount of time invested in advance can save a great deal of time on every occasion the task is required to be undertaken. The template may even contain the company details section, thus alleviating the need to retype this on each occasion. It may be that several different versions of the company details could be stored and used according to the level or category of vacancy to be filled.

Inclusion of minimum criteria
It is important that the minimum criteria for the job are included in the advertisement. The purpose of the job advertisement is not to generate high numbers of applicants but rather to generate sufficient numbers of *suitable* applicants between which a decision can be made. Job advertisements that yield 200 applicants for one vacancy should not be regarded as successful adverts. Some poor soul has got to read all of those applications.

Acquiring details of the applicants
In order for management to gain maximum time advantage, applicants should be discouraged from sending in a lengthy CV at this stage. Reading CVs is not a pastime that I have particularly enjoyed over the years. It is difficult to extract the salient data from a document that has been laid out to tell you what the applicant wants you to know rather than what you actually want to know. It is difficult to take in *any* information from a CV, and once a recruiter has read ten or so, they tend to merge into each other. Details other than the basics, which have probably been extracted and listed, will undoubtedly be lost.

Another point, of course, is that in order to evaluate a CV, management time is being taken up. But saving management time is one of the prime reasons for utilising the computer in the first place. Every job advertisement should therefore contain a statement asking individuals to phone for an application form and *not* to send a CV.

At the time of initial enquiry the details of each applicant can be entered into the system in an applicant details table (see Table 14, page 72). With the exception of the vacancy number and applicant identification number, this requires no more input than courtesy would demand of a manual system by which an application form was sent in an addressed envelope.

Once an applicant's details have been entered in the system

all sorts of data analysis and report production become possible – not least of which is the production of a personalised letter and application form (see next section). This should be the last time that anyone has to type the applicants' details until a successful candidate is entered onto the formal HR system.

The application form

Having identified the criteria for a position, some of which may be very easy to achieve, it is possible to produce an individualised job application form for each vacancy. Indeed, a form can be produced for each applicant.

By the time the system has progressed far enough for details of an applicant to be sought there will be sufficient information on the computer for each applicant to receive an individualised application form. The form could already contain an applicant number, the applicant's name and address, the vacancy details (including the job number) and, most importantly, a section that asks whether the applicant can fulfil the minimum requirements of the job.

The section could be in the form of the table set out as Table 15.

The personal details section of the application form could also be produced in a tick-box format. This will allow for a computer scanner to read the application form and store data of gender, ethnic origin, age, etc, in addition to the responses for the knockout questions relating to the minimum criteria.

This data will also enable the comprehensive monitoring of

Table 14

| Job vacancy number |
| Applicant identifier number |
| Title field eg MR MRS etc. |
| Forename |
| Surname |
| Address 1 |
| Address 2 |
| Town |
| Postcode |
| Daytime phone |
| Evening phone |

Table 15

	The following questions represent the minimum standards of ability or achievement that we are seeking for this position. Please indicate as honestly as you can whether you fulfil the criteria set out below. Please circle yes or no to enter a value. Have you	
1	A degree in mechanical engineering?	Yes No
2	Managed a production environment manufacturing perishable products for at least two years?	Yes No
3	Managed a production environment with responsibility for quality assurance, production and packaging for at least two years?	Yes No
4	Directly supervised non-engineering and engineering personnel in a manufacturing process for a minimum of two years?	Yes No
5	Please quote salary earned in last job	£
	If you fulfil our minimum requirement we will ask you to submit a full CV. Please do not submit a CV at this stage	

recruitment patterns and equal opportunities aspects.

It is not strictly necessary for the data to be scanned into a computer: that of course depends on the size of the organisation and the number of vacancies being dealt with. The data could readily be entered into the system manually, using a computer screen pro forma which mirrored the hard copy and which required the person inputting to select 'Y' or 'N' or enter a value in the appropriate field. Only the reader can decide which method is viable for his or her own organisation. Scanners typically take 15 to 20 seconds to scan an A4 sheet.

Advantages of producing an individualised letter and application form include

- the ease with which data can be handled
- the ability to determine what data is supplied

- the ability to decide who meets the minimum criteria
- generating a professional image to all applicants who may well also be customers
- ongoing data analysis.

Progressing the application

Up to this point the computer is holding data about a number of applicants for each vacancy that is current. Now the computer can start to aid the decision-making processes of recruitment. We need to set up a data table that will log applicant progression. Most applicants will never have more than one entry in this table.

The required data fields will be:

- applicant number
- date
- minimum met
- action.

Various levels of sophistication can be achieved in the management of this table, but the outcome will be the same. The table will control reports produced by the system that either advance the application or send a reject letter.

The initial entry can be generated by the computer itself if the user has adequate knowledge to write a small macro (mini program) that recognises when the scanned or entered application data does not have a corresponding applicant number in the progression table. The macro would then enter the date and a new applicant number. It does not need to enter the job number because that can be linked via the applicant details table. The macro could then establish whether the minimum criteria had been established, and enter a 'Y' or 'N' in the 'Minimum met' data field. When the system is subsequently asked to produce the reports for today, any applicants with an 'N' entered in this field would automatically be sent a personalised reject letter which could extract the address details and the vacancy details from the data stored in the appropriate tables.

(If you are wondering how the program decides whether to enter a 'Y' or an 'N' in the 'Minimum met' field, it would do so by running a query based on 'IF' statements that used the following logic.

IF: Criterion 1 or Criterion 2 or Criterion 3 or Criterion 4 = 'N', or Criterion 5 is greater than allowed, Then enter 'N', Otherwise enter 'Y')

The 'Y' or 'N' could equally well be entered manually – but would of course be prone to human error.

The entry of a 'Y' would trigger a letter inviting the applicant to send a CV.

In the actual selection process this may well be the first time that management time has been involved: substantially fewer CVs will need reading, all of which will at least reach the minimum standard for the job.

Although this table appears to be quite small in terms of the number of fields, it is the key to the progression and management of vacancies. The action field can be predetermined for the acceptable entries that can be made by setting up a table with possible occurrences and a code for each. The codes could be entered via a drop-down list box showing the full entry phrase, so that a click with the mouse button will be all that is needed for the value to be entered.

The categories in Table 16 (page 76) are only guidelines: the user can choose whatever stages are appropriate to the required process. However, whatever the entries, a code value entered in the table will trigger a number of reports.

Progression reports

The use of the word 'reports' is a feature of RDBMS. But for the purposes of this section a 'standard report' can also describe a standardised letter to individual applicants which will be sent according to the entry in the code field. An advantage of using such a coded system is that candidates cannot be lost in the system or left without a reply to each stage of the process until they are finally rejected or appointed.

Although very little data is actually held in the records of this table, the reports associated with it can be manifold. With a little thought, tables can be created that allow interviews to be scheduled, records to be produced of which

Table 16

Acceptable entry	code
Reject after CV (no interview)	r1
Invite for 1st interview	I1
Reject after 1st interview	r2
Invite to assessment centre	As
Reject after assessment centre	r3
Invite for 2nd interview	I2
Reject after 2nd interview	r4
Offer	of

managers have interviewed which candidates, and invitations for interview letters sent out.

At any time reports can be run off from the system which can represent a snapshot of information relating to current vacancies. For example, at the touch of a button reports could be set up to give an up-to-the-minute account of the:

- number of current vacancies
- number of applicants per vacancy
- number of CVs requested/received
- number of telephone enquiries that did not yield a returned application
- present stage of each vacancy
- number of recruitment initiatives that yielded/did not yield a successful candidate.

This represents only a few of the possible summarised calculated outputs that such a system could give in relation to the recruitment statistics.

Terms and conditions

As a final stage of the recruitment process we need to ensure that terms and conditions are offered to the candidate that are appropriate to the job. In most organisations the conditions are consistent within the different levels of employment but may vary from one level to another. To ensure that consistency among peers is maintained, the system could generate a standard report/letter which ensures that the same package is offered to employees of equivalent level or type of job. The job details, location, grade, salary and immediately senior person, together with other variable data, would be contained within the data tables developed for the system, so each set of terms and conditions would be accurately but individually produced.

Data Protection

The Data Protection Act requires that information pinpointing individuals should be held only for as long as is necessary to undertake the purpose of the data application. In terms of the recruitment process – except for some high-risk posts where security vetting takes place – it ought to be possible to dispense with personal details as soon as the recruitment campaign to fill a particular vacancy has been successfully completed. But for the purposes of analysis and management control we would not want to dispense with all of the accumulated data. All that is necessary to purge from the data tables is the applicant's forename, surname, and the first line of the address. The rest of the data – including the general location – may be of benefit in the analysis of data.

Benefits of a computerised recruitment system

The reader may well think at this stage that a lot of effort has gone into developing a system which could be managed quite easily without taking such actions.

This is true in part. But there are many benefits to be gained from having such a useful body of data building up on an ongoing basis. Some of the data useful to the reports suggested herein may not have been specifically indicated as essential to obtain – but it can easily be added in. It is very much the decision of the individual which data fields should be included over and above those suggested.

Some form of overall cost per vacancy may be important to your organisation. The matter can be addressed by adding calculations that estimate interview costs, interview venue costs (if appropriate), advertising costs, etc. It is easy to produce reports by vacancy, by department, by region, by job type or by any other meaningful parameter.

The monitoring of equal opportunities in recruitment is

very easy and comprehensive with a source database such as described. Not only can direct measures of issues such as gender or race be analysed and reported upon – so can indirect issues such as identifying whether adverts are attracting candidates from areas of one predominant culture. Age profiles of candidates can be analysed against ages of successful candidates. Disability discrimination monitoring can be undertaken.

All of this can be produced on a regular or *ad hoc* basis as and when required by the organisation. The greatest benefit is that at the time the reports are run off they are right up to date and accurate.

A further feature of relational databases is the ability to track through a number of tables linking data from tables actually perhaps two or three links removed from each other. For example: imagine that an organisation has been accused of discriminating against a particular ethnic group in its recruitment at one location.

By linking data gained from the job details form (to gain the location) to data from the applicant details table (to get ethnic origin data) and to data in the vacancy progression table (to get details at which stage applicants were rejected or dropped out), a comprehensive analysis of such a claim could be made. Furthermore, if data indicating which managers had undertaken interviews has been stored (it is necessary as a primary data source for arranging interviews), it would be possible to undertake such an analysis by individual manager/interviewer. All this would provide tangible evidence on which to judge the accusation, and act accordingly.

It is just this sort of problem, which comes to light every now and then, that is an absolute nightmare to try to investigate fairly if such a database has not been built up. Thus in addition to the functional control that such a computerised recruitment database can give, it can also help to manage the overall process, giving up-to-the-minute recruitment information and the ability to interrogate the data when problems arise. By being able to interrogate data in so many ways, the sources of problems such as high labour turnover can be thoroughly analysed and investigated. And budget overspends can be isolated down to the real culprits.

The benefits of computerising the recruitment management process outweigh the time taken to develop such a system and to make it relatively easy to use for the people who input and extract the information. You will doubtless be able to think of other aspects that would be useful to you in your own organisation. The outputs of the system are limited only by the user's imagination and the data fields chosen. More data fields and tables can be added at any time. As long as the data tables can be logically linked, information can be extracted.

5

MANAGING THE

EMPLOYMENT OF STAFF

This chapter looks at ways that the duration of a job and the employment of a job holder can be enhanced by the use of computer-based HRM techniques. It also looks at ways of utilising data that may well be held on an existing computerised HRM system, as well as making some suggestions on other ways that a computer can be used, including the exporting of data that is already stored in an HRM system into a spreadsheet or database application for further analysis. We shall also look at introducing some further parameters to job identification techniques as a way of sensibly analysing data and planning careers (although career-planning is itself covered in a later chapter).

The chapter is not meant as a critique of computerised HRM systems; nor is it a critique of best HRM practice. Like other chapters in the book, it is meant as a stimulus to the reader – to awaken ideas that can be utilised within the reader's own organisation. Some of the ideas and techniques proposed may be counter to the practices of the reader's organisation, but they may nevertheless provide food for thought.

The previous chapter dealt with the use of computers in relation to the recruitment of employees. In that chapter mention was made of job analysis and job evaluation. The theme of the chapter was to adopt some of the principles of the management by objectives (MbO) philosophy of Peter Drucker.[1] I propose to continue talking about this philosophy for much of the early part of this chapter.

The chapter will look at ways the computer can aid in job evaluation, contract and employment package management, complying with legislation, and in monitoring organisational HRM processes.

Job evaluation

Job evaluation is a contentious process in many organisations, and one that can involve a great deal of management time and require a large amount of money to implement. There are many consultancy firms that can come into an organisation to undertake a thorough job evaluation analysis. The whole process of job evaluation is regarded by many HRM practitioners as subjective and unnecessary. They see it as restricting the organisation by not allowing the employment of individuals at market or premium rates, which appear to fall outside the evaluated grades of the organisation. It has to be recognised that such views exist, and that the technique is not in vogue for many sectors.

Job evaluation is included within this chapter in recognition of the future possibility of European legislation, currently under discussion, which will require an employer to demonstrate that there are systems within the organisation to ensure equality of pay for equal jobs. The onus will be on the employer to prove that there are such systems, and not on the employee to prove that there are not. If a company cannot exhibit such systems, the case will be awarded to the employee.

This section centres on possible ways for an organisation to undertake its own evaluation of jobs and to rate them in terms of their value to the organisation. It is the comprehensiveness of the salary grade matrix, which will be discussed later, that determines the applicability of the job evaluations to the market forces affecting the organisation.

There must be countless ways in which criteria for job evaluation can be established. The use of identified job competencies is one example. The example below uses the MbO philosophy of Peter Drucker which, loosely paraphrased, states that what is important to measure about a job is its output. It is what job holders are accountable for achieving

Table 17

SALES	PROFIT	PEOPLE
DEFINE POLICY	DEFINE POLICY	DEFINE POLICY
DEFINE STRATEGY	DEFINE STRATEGY	DEFINE STRATEGY
DEFINE TACTICS	DEFINE TACTICS	DEFINE TACTICS
IMPLEMENT TACTICS	REPORTING	MANAGING
GENERATE REVENUE	SUPPORT	SUPERVISING
ACHIEVING	ACHIEVING	INTERFACING
		SELECTING

CLIENTS	EQUIPMENT	COSTS
DEFINE POLICY	DEFINE POLICY	DEFINE POLICY
DEFINE STRATEGY	DEFINE STRATEGY	DEFINE STRATEGY
DEFINE TACTICS	DEFINE TACTICS	DEFINE TACTICS
GENERATE	PROCURING	CONTROL
MANAGE	SUPERVISING	REPORTING
SUPPORT	REPORTING	
CONTACT		
telephone		
face to face		

PRODUCT		SKILLS
DEFINE POLICY		PROFESSIONAL
DEFINE STRATEGY		TECHNICAL
DEFINE TACTICS		SPECIALIST
DEVELOPMENT		VERBAL
DELIVERY		NUMERIC
REPORTING		MANUAL
		ADMIN
		WRITTEN
		KEYBOARD
		UNSOCIAL HOURS ELEMENT

that is important, not what they need in order to be able to do it. In the case of job evaluation, therefore, it is the outputs and the degree of accountability that are used to measure the value of a job to an organisation. The value could also be assessed from the point of view of the consequence to the organisation of the job holder's not achieving this aspect of their accountability. Humble (1972)[2] discerned the main stages of the process of MbO as the identification of strategic, tactical and unit objectives which lead to the identification of broad accountability areas and key result areas. It is the last two that can be utilised within this model of job evaluation.

The MbO model shows that there are approximately six or seven broad accountability areas for a job or even for an organisation. Table 17 features seven broad accountability areas. These areas will change from organisation to organisation, but they will be consistent throughout each organisation for the purpose of evaluating jobs.

The fictitious organisation that represents our example is a computer training organisation that develops training courses for commercially available software and then sells the training courses to other organisations usually by requiring people to attend a public or in-house programme.

The broad accountability areas that are being used are: 'Sales', 'Clients', 'Profit', 'People', 'Equipment', 'Costs', and 'Product'. There is a further area that assesses the skill level required to undertake the job against a set of parameters, and

Table 18

BROAD ACCOUNTABILITY AREAS	JOB EVALUATION MATRIX RATING = I VERY LOW ----9 VERY HIGH					
SALES	SALE DIR	DIV S.MGR	REG S.MGR	ACC MGR	ACC EXEC	DEPT ADMIN
DEFINE POLICY	9	6	0	0	0	0
DEFINE STRATEGY	9	6	4	0	3	0
DEFINE TACTICS	9	6	4	0	5	0
IMPLEMENT TACTICS	7	5	6	8	6	0
GENERATE REVENUE	9	7	7	7	7	0
CLIENTS						
DEFINE POLICY	9	6	0	0	0	0
DEFINE STRATEGY	9	6	5	5	2	0
DEFINE TACTICS	7	6	6	7	6	0
GENERATE	5	7	8	8	6	0
MANAGE	3	6	8	8	0	0
SUPPORT	3	2	3	4	6	4
CONTACT	6	5	7	7	9	5
telephone	3	2	3	3	3	3
face to face	3	3	4	4	6	2
PROFIT						
DEFINE POLICY	9	0	0	0	0	0
DEFINE STRATEGY	9	3	3	0	0	0
DEFINE TACTICS	9	7	6	6	3	0
REPORTING	3	4	6	7	5	8
SUPPORT	6	9	6	4	9	5
ACHIEVING	9	9	7	7	5	0
PEOPLE						
DEFINE POLICY	8	0	0	0	0	0
DEFINE STRATEGY	8	5	4	0	0	0
DEFINE TACTICS	8	6	4	0	0	0
MANAGING	8	7	6	0	0	0
SUPERVISING	5	6	6	3	0	0
INTERFACING	8	8	8	8	9	9
SELECTING	8	7	4	0	0	0

Table 18 cont.

EQUIPMENT	SALE DIR	DIV S.MGR	REG S.MGR	ACC MGR	ACC EXEC	DEPT ADMIN
DEFINE POLICY	2	0	0	0	0	0
DEFINE STRATEGY	2	0	0	0	0	0
DEFINE TACTICS	2	0	0	0	0	0
PROCURING	1	0	0	0	0	6
SUPERVISING	2	2	2	3	2	3
REPORTING	2	3	3	3	3	3

COSTS						
DEFINE POLICY	9	0	0	0	0	0
DEFINE STRATEGY	9	5	0	0	0	0
DEFINE TACTICS	7	6	6	0	0	0
CONTROL	7	7	7	0	3	0
REPORTING	4	4	4	3	3	9

PRODUCT						
DEFINE POLICY	7	0	0	0	0	0
DEFINE STRATEGY	7	4	0	0	0	0
DEFINE TACTICS	6	6	4	0	0	0
DEVELOPMENT	4	3	3	2	0	0
DELIVERY	1	0	0	0	0	0
REPORTING	2	3	4	4	3	3

SKILLS							
	PROFESSIONAL	9	6	5	0	3	3
	TECHNICAL	2	0	0	0	0	0
	SPECIALIST	8	7	7	7	5	5
	VERBAL	8	7	7	7	7	5
	NUMERIC	3	3	3	3	3	6
	MANUAL	0	0		0	0	5
	ADMIN	6	6	5	5	3	9
	WRITTEN	6	6	5	5	5	7
	KEYBOARD	0	0	0	0	0	6
UNSOCIAL HOURS ELEMENT		9	4		3	0	0

319	233	198	150	139	106
M	L	K	J	I	G

also a component that assesses the unsocial hours component of each job.

Each of the broad accountability areas is subdivided into key result areas (KRAs) which each job can be measured against. These need to reflect the common parameters against which each job can in some way be evaluated. Table 17 shows the KRAs for each of the broad accountabilities.

There is nothing magical about the KRAs identified – indeed, they may not all be applicable to other organisations. What is important is that they represent the accountability areas and the key result areas that are valued by the organisation for which they are being used. In the table the reader will see that the broad areas have a number of components in common to each – notably the accountability for defining policy, strategy and tactics. In addition to these, each area has at least three other key result areas that measure the employees' level of accountability in each area. Every employee is rated against each of the identified KRAs on a scale of zero to nine, depending on the degree of accountability within his or her job for each factor. Table 18 shows a number of jobs rated against the accountability areas identified for the organisation. The whole organisation can be rated against each of the KRAs. Obviously, some jobs will score zeroes in certain areas and high scores in other areas.

It could be argued that a felt-fair method of job evaluation might be used, especially within departments. But felt-fair methods can start to fall apart when seeking to compare jobs across departments. Given the pending European legislation or even current UK equal opportunities legislation, a simple low-cost factor-analysis system such as the one illustrated here could save an organisation considerable time and money in the event of a court action.

There are two major ways in which the computerisation of the technique can be achieved: either on a spreadsheet or on a RDBMS. The spreadsheet is the easier option in terms of computer skills. However, it is also the one that will give less long-term analytical opportunity.

To undertake the exercise on a spreadsheet it is a case of building up a column of headings that represent the broad accountability areas and the key result areas (KRAs) of the organisation, as in Table 18, and then rating each job type within the organisation against the KRAs on the chosen scale. Zero to nine has been used in the example in order to have a conventional ten-point scale and also because it only requires the input of one digit. The column for each job can then be added by using the 'Sum' (Σ) function of the spreadsheet. This will identify a points

Table 19

BETWEEN	0	39	C
BETWEEN	40	59	D
BETWEEN	60	69	E
BETWEEN	70	89	F
BETWEEN	90	109	G
BETWEEN	110	129	H
BETWEEN	130	149	I
BETWEEN	150	169	J
BETWEEN	170	209	K
BETWEEN	210	249	L
ABOVE	250		M

score for each job. And if this is how the organisation identifies the rating of the job, no more need be done. If, as is more normal, however, jobs are allocated grade letters, the built-in 'Look up' function in the spreadsheet can be utilised to convert the number to a grade. This involves entering the maximum points rating for a letter grade in an area of the current spreadsheet with the corresponding grade next to it.

The last two columns of Table 19 could represent the range of values needed to be stored in a spreadsheet 'Look up' table area.

A 'Look up' function has three parameters that need to be entered:

- a cell containing the value to be converted (in table 18b this would be a cell with the numerical total of points awarded to the job)
- the range of cells in which the corresponding points value and alphabetical value can be found (the last two columns of Table 19)
- the column number from this range that is returned to the formulated cell.

The spreadsheet will look up the letter within which range the numerical value falls – so a value of 61 would return an 'E' grade, 89 would return an 'F' grade.

The formulated cell in the example would be the cell under the numerical points value for each grade. With the formula copied across the row, each row would display the appropriate letter value.

Table 20

JOB NUMBER
DATE
POLICY
STRATEGY
TACTICS
IMPLEMENT TACTICS
GENERATE REVENUE

By following the instructions for the function in the particular spreadsheet package being used, a formula can be entered under the points total that will look up the corresponding grade letter.

The value of 39 in Table 19 will need to be changed to zero to prevent the computer from giving an 'Error' message when a value of less than 39 is entered. This is an example of complying with the needs of the computer rather than the realities of life. It is unlikely that any job will score lower than 39 points, but it is possible. What the computer will now understand from this table is that any value less than 39 will be returned as a grade 'C'. This is the lowest grade available in the system. It is better to build in this safeguard than to confuse users with an 'Error' message that is effectively meaningless.

This spreadsheet method is useful if there are relatively few jobs within an organisation. The matrix format of the report is also useful, but it could just as easily be produced by a database with the added advantage that the data could be used for relational analysis. It may also be useful when seeking employees for career moves within the organisation. It would also be possible to have a job evaluation history, which could show the evolution of a job and how it has changed, with a minimum of data entry and storage space.

To set up the job evaluation process on a RDBMS it is necessary to think through the structure and number of data tables that are required. It is likely that each broad accountability area will need a data table; it will also need a relational field. Think back to Chapter 2, where it was suggested that there should be a job details table that would include a job identification number. It would be a good idea to use this same number as the relational field in the broad accountability tables, together with a date: the date field should also be a primary indexing key unique to the table. In this way a unique set of values can be entered for each broad accountability area for each time a job is assessed. New key results areas can be added through time, if necessary. If new KRAs are added, each new job evaluation must include the new KRAs to give consistency across all jobs. New KRAs should therefore not be added lightly.

Table 20 (page 87) shows the possible data field structure for a sales accountability table.

Similar tables need to be set up for each accountability area, ensuring that the features to be measured within the KRA are included. This approach is actually more simple than it sounds. Once it has been set up it can be used time and again for every job in the organisation. Each factor can be analysed separately, if necessary, and the statistics produced can demonstrate the fairness of the system and the fact that it is related to the requirements of the job, not the skills of the person actually doing the job. A person who is overqualified for a job would therefore not be paid more because of his or her overqualification. The reader may well be thinking that this limits the ability of an organisation to reward individuals for acquiring skills as a result of career-planning. But any such payment can be undertaken via a development review. Payments of this kind are based on identified skills acquisition and individual merit, and as such are permissible within equal opportunities policies provided that like achievements are treated equally.

The contract of employment

The nature of the employment contract is such that it is implicit unless otherwise stated. This fact has been the downfall of many tribunal cases where contractual issues have been at stake. Although there is a move toward single-status contracts within some organisations, it is still a far from universal practice; perhaps it never will be. This said, most organisations have at least one or two types of employment contracts offering different terms and conditions of employment. The differences between the contracts are usually associated with the level of the jobs within the organisation. Current employment legislation requires that an employee is informed of the basic terms and conditions of employment within eight weeks of the commencement of employment. Many employers issue the terms and conditions with the offer of employment, which seems logical, for the prospective employee needs to know what it is he or she is being offered.

Because the terms and conditions are usually consistent across grade and department, a standard report-type document can be generated by a database system which ensures that all contracts issued to like jobs at like grades and levels of responsibility are the same.

There are a number of ways in which the generation of this output report could be triggered, depending on the sophistication of the system. At the highest level of sophistication the contract could be automatically produced by the HR information system on the input of new employee details. Each new employee would be designated a job, and on identification of the job the terms and conditions and major features of the contract would be produced by the system. Other varying levels of sophistication can be achieved, depending on the utilisation of IT. The purpose of the IT system is to aid and enhance rather than to be an exercise in automating the processes. Individual readers alone can decide what is viable for their own organisations. Probably the most realistic proposal for many organisations – if a database approach is to be used – is to have the features of the terms and conditions and other contract clauses stored in a database, and to produce reports based on each employment. To achieve this, a contract of employment would need to be viewed as a series of modules which could be joined together as one report. Each module can be established as a data table with the following data fields:

- job category (manual, supervisory, management, executive, etc)
- grade-range high and grade-range low (the lowest and highest permissible grades that the feature can be assigned to)
- date reviewed

- statement (eg: The normal hours of work for this job will be 9.00 am to 5.30 pm Monday to Friday, with an hour lunch-break to be taken unpaid and at a time agreed with the immediate supervisor).

A number of data records can be built up that represent the full range of possibilities within the organisation. A query statement can then be developed which prompts for the required parameters of the job and then produces an appropriate contract. The query would in fact require the parameters or conditions that triggered the data statement to be included or excluded from the report. That is, if the above hours of work applied to all grades below grade 'G', then an entry of ' < G' would have to be placed in the query table to trigger the appropriate response. This would in fact select all grades from A to F. Similarly, all other statements applicable to the job could be included in the query. By also linking the query to a job number in the job details table, the location, title and grade can be automatically added.

This method of building a contract of employment is outlined here to show how it can be done. It is likely that if such a technique were to be used, it would be developed by an advanced user of RDBMS technology. There is a distinct danger of overcomplicating a process with technology just because it is possible. Nevertheless, once set up and tested, it would always produce the correct contract.

Let us return to the former premise that there are in fact only a few different types of contract in most organisations, regardless of the number of employees. It is just as simple to have the process set up on a word-processing function linked to a mail merge data facility on which the contractee's details can be stored and merged with a standard contract for the grade level or job type of the new employee. A word of caution, however. Although the automated technique using the database may appear to be cumbersome, remember that once it is set up it will reproduce the same result from the same input data every time. The word-processing approach, which relies on human decision-making, is on the other hand susceptible to error every time it is used. Which technique to use really depends on the perceived level of risk the organisation sees within the process. If the organisation issues a large number of contracts as a result of rapid growth or high labour turnover, an automated approach may be beneficial. Conversely, if the number of contracts issued is minimal, a manual system will probably work best so long as it includes a checking mechanism.

Managing menu-type terms and conditions

A growing number of organisations have introduced a menu approach to the employment contract whereby employees can, to some extent, determine the make-up of their own contract of employment. For example: employees might opt whether or not to belong to a private health scheme, an option that may be open just to themselves, to themselves and their spouses or to the whole family. Similarly, employees may be able to buy extra holidays or trade some of their holiday entitlement for extra salary. One week of holiday might (for instance) equate to approximately 2 per cent of the overall salary. Some way of reconciling these variable benefits needs to be established by an organisation. In a small organisation it might be achievable on a spreadsheet, although it would soon become unwieldy. A RDBMS would manage the process far more comprehensively.

The normal way that a menu system approach is operated is for employees to select any of a number of options within the work contract. These may include features such as private health schemes, dental insurance, child-care vouchers, different pension scheme conditions, life assurance and holidays. Such schemes have to be precise in their structure and must be rigorously enforced. Many schemes calculate the cost of the chosen benefit and deduct it from an overall individual personal points allowance. This method lends itself very well to the use of RDBMS. Most of the data required will already be held within the main HR information system and can be downloaded if necessary to a PC.

A 'flexibenefits table' could be set up which contains the individual benefit names and their costs to the employee. Table 21 (page 92) shows a table of this kind.

Such a table would then be used as the source table for the flexible benefits management application.

One other source table would be needed: an amount table.

Table 21
FLEXIBENEFITS TABLE

BENEFIT	CODE	COST
PRIVATE HEALTH SELF ONLY	PHS	360
PRIVATE HEALTH SELF & SPOUSE	PH2	720
PRIVATE HEALTH FAMILY	PHF	1000
EXTRA HOLIDAY PER DAY	EXHOL	=SALARY * 004
LESS HOLIDAY PER DAY	LESSHOL	=SALARY * 004
CHILD-CARE VOUCHERS/ CHILD	VOUCH	1000
ENHANCED PENSION 1/60	PENS60	500
ENHANCED PENSION 1/55	PENS55	750
ENHANCED PENSION 1/50	PENS50	1000
DENTAL SELF	DENT1	200
DENTAL SELF & SPOUSE	DENT2	400
LIFE ASSURANCE	ASSU	240

This would show the amount available for each employee to spend within his or her benefits package. The amount could be fixed for all employees; it might be conditional on employee grade; or it could be a percentage of salary. Whichever system is chosen, the table would need a date field as the annual reference date, and an amount field per grade field or a percentage of salary field. Any form or report that was subsequently produced could calculate or enter the amount available to each employee on an individual report form.

A data input table can be defined that includes the employee number and the benefits that the employee has opted to include within the contract for the current employment year. This table could be developed in at least two ways. One way would obviate the need for the flexibenefit table described above but would make possible analysis of the data less comprehensive and input more lengthy. A table similar to Table 21 is set up to include a yes or no input option against each possible benefit. This would mean that an entry had to be made for every employee against every possible option, thus taking more time and more memory space. A better way to achieve the task is to use the flexibenefits table as the source table and a new selected benefits table as the control table for the application. The selected benefits table would need to include the employee number, date, and the benefit code and benefit cost for each benefit chosen. This may seem

Figure 5
BENEFIT INPUT FORM

employee number	employee surname	forename	job title	location	department
1234	BROWNING	SARAH	SECRETARY	BRIGHTON	FINANCE

ALLOWANCE =	£1500

YEAR	EMPLOYEE NUMBER	HOLIDAY DAYS	BENEFIT CODE	BENEFIT COST	RUNNING TOTAL
1997	1234		VOUCH	1000	1000
1997	1234		PHS	360	1360
1997	1234	2	EXHOL	120	1480
				BALANCE	£20

a lot, but by using multiform input options – see individual RDBMS packages for how to achieve this – it is possible to enter the data by selecting from drop-down boxes once the correct employee has been found. Figure 5 shows how this form might appear.

Although all of the information will appear on one screen, there are in fact two forms on the screen: the master form, identified by the shaded area, and the subform, which includes the rest of the data fields. Once the form appears on the screen, the user can either type in the employee name or number or scroll through until the correct employee is found. By setting this up as a drop-down scroll box, the correct employee can be very quickly found. The bottom area of the box will show the entries already made for this employee at previous times. The user can quickly move to the last entry by clicking on the solid arrowhead key ➡ and then onto a blank record. The form can be set up to input the current employee number and date year, the holiday years can be entered (if appropriate), and the benefit code can be entered by selecting from a drop-down scroll box. By adopting this method, keystroke entry is kept to a minimum, a running total can be kept, and the system can prevent overspend entries from being accepted.

Building up a data table of benefit choices in this way

enables a subsequent analysis of cost by option, department, grade, etc, to be very easily developed which can give accurate information upon which to judge the viability of each of the options and, indeed, the scheme in general.

Grade and salary matrix

The precise form of a grade matrix depends on the organisation. Each grade band needs to be wide enough to accommodate and satisfy the needs of the individuals within each band. The salary levels need to reflect the range of salaries at which the organisation will be able to recruit the staff that it requires, paying the right price for the person. Without a salary matrix set against grades for the job there is likely to be salary drift upwards, thus creating a situation where more is paid than is necessary. Individual merit payments or performance-related payments can be paid in addition to salary if desired and if appropriate.

As for the matrix and the value added by the computer, it is the relationship between the grades and the incremental points within grades that the RDBMS can help most in.

Most salary matrices have characteristics that can be computerised, and with the amendment of a key value each year (or whenever reviews take place), the whole process can be updated with the minimum number of entries. By undertaking the process in this way, any calculation process that

Table 22

VALID	1.1.98					
GRADE	BENCH	1	2	3	4	5
D	6000	6300	6600	6900	7200	7500
E	7380	7749	8118	8487	8856	9225
F	9077	9531	9985	10439	10893	11347
G	11165	11723	12282	12840	13398	13957
H	13733	14420	15107	15793	16480	17166
I	16892	17736	18581	19426	20270	21115
J	20777	21816	22855	23893	24932	25971

involves the salary amount can instantly be updated. Table 22 shows an example of a salary matrix.

In Table 22 all cells are related to the amount entered in the bench value for grade 'D'. Each incremental point within the grades is 105 per cent of the previous point, and each grade band bench value increases by 123 per cent of the previous grade bench, thus allowing a small overlap in each grade. The example can be extended for as many grades as required and as many increments as required, although in the case of the increased incremental points the grade band differential relationship would need to be altered to a figure different from 123 per cent. By maintaining these relationships a degree of consistency and fairness is arrived at in the salary structure. On the computer it is only a matter of changing the bench value in grade 'D' and the whole matrix will update itself. So if a 3 per cent general pay increase is awarded by entering 6180 in the bench cell of grade 'D', the whole table will update by the same percentage increase.

Although the sample matrix table is shown in the form produced by a spreadsheet, a similar process can be undertaken within the RDBMS and each value could thus be read from the table containing the new matrix. This is a particularly efficient way to undertake the database method because only the one value needs to be entered into the computer: the rest are calculated amounts that can be produced by the computer, satisfying the requirement to let the computer do any calculation that it has the ability to do. To retain historical data it will be necessary to enter a date with the benchmark amount, so allowing data to refer back to previous years if a comparison is required. Each employee's current salary would thus be aligned to the latest grade and incremental point value in the salary matrix 'Look up' table, or that of any year that was required.

A process like the one described here enables the organisation and the HRM function to retain simple control over salary structures.

Maintaining the staff records

It is not the main purpose of this book to discuss the setting up of a staff record-keeping system such as those now commercially available. Nevertheless, it is worth a few lines to stress the need to ensure that the system is kept up to date. Data exported, or more correctly, copied, to spreadsheets or other packages for further analysis needs to be as up to date as possible in order that the information generated should be as accurate as possible. It is essential, therefore, that the accountabilities for inputting data need to be defined as a specific part of employees' jobs. In the past when many more personnel functions were centralised and computer systems tended to be centralised as well, input was largely by data input clerks, at least in organisations where there was enough data to warrant it. Smaller organisations tended to have manual systems anyway. Because it was someone's whole job, or a major part of it, data was mostly up to date on entry, always supposing that the input documentation had been sent through. With the advent of the powerful PC-based machines, networking, and the devolution of many HRM functions to the line, together with the emergence of easy-to-use software, data input is now often undertaken as a small part of the job of a person who has little to do with the HRM function at any other time. The operation of a computerised HRIS has also become viable and desirable for comparatively small businesses. But inputting such data may not be seen as a priority for the employee who inputs the data, or for his or her supervisor. So it is important for HRM to seek ways to ensure that the data is as up to date as possible. The problem is not unique to HRM: it is a likely symptom of flatter, decentralised organisations such as those that are developing now. It can have similar effects on other business functions that now rely on other areas of the business – over which they have no line authority – for the basic data they need for the management of their own sphere of the organisation.

The system can be made to assist in its own management by checking whether input has occurred from a specific location within a given time-span, or whether a complete set of records has been set up for an individual. For example: a new employee should not be entered onto the payroll until all of the other personal details have been entered into the system. This is probably a feature of most record-keeping software systems anyway – many require an employee to be assigned to a job before he or she can in fact be paid.

Problems may arise when a payroll system is separate from the HRIS, but even then an interface program can be written to check that each system has the data it requires before a payment can be made. A more likely scenario is the degradation of data in areas such as absence monitoring or any similar process that needs periodic updating. Here again the computer system can, to some extent, be self-managing. The system can be asked to produce a set of reports that show the HRM department, and local department managers, types of data that have not had entries made in them for predefined periods of time. It may be, for instance, that a department is expected to log attendance details weekly. It is a simple matter for the system to search its data entry records and identify by department, location, or any other sensible grouping, where data has not been entered for the specified period. It could even identify the average time-lapse between previous entry dates and report on those where entries have not been made within the average data entry period. This is not infallible, because there may genuinely be no entries to be made, but at least it brings the matter to light and enables HRM to show that it is managing the system.

The information generated by any computer system can only ever be as good as the quality of the data input into the system. It is crucial therefore that input staff understand this and also that where possible the system seeks to be self-auditing. Ways of effecting this have been discussed in other areas of this book. Setting default entry values or defining acceptable entry codes and rejecting any others are two ways that can assist a system to self-manage itself. If unacceptable entries cannot be put into the database in the first place, then a consistency of data entry occurs that at least fits the recognised patterns. Of course even this does not prevent an operator's keying in an acceptable but incorrect piece of data. Beware! Incorrect entries can lead to problems with the Data Protection legislation. This should nevertheless not stop the computerisation of employee data. It has so many advantages.

References

1   DRUCKER P. 'The practice of management' in L. Mullins (ed.), *Management and Organisational Behaviour*, 4th edn, London, Pitman, 1996, p. 447.

2   HUMBLE J.W. *Management by Objectives*, Management Publications Ltd for The British Institute of Management, 1972, p. 32.

6

PERFORMANCE AND DEVELOPMENT APPRAISAL MANAGEMENT

This chapter is closely linked with Chapter 8, which is concerned with succession planning. The two have nonetheless been kept separate because it is possible to undertake the functions of this chapter without going as far as the succession-planning techniques described in Chapter 7.

Like previous chapters this chapter offers a model that is not put forward as my personal, definitive view of the topic but rather as one that is both practical and practicable for appraisal management.

Appraisal of any kind has always been a controversial subject within the personnel and HRM function. Techniques have ranged from not doing it to participative appraisal, 360-degree appraisal to non-participative performance assessment in which the appraiser tells the appraisee what rating has been given. All of these techniques can doubtless still be found in use in various organisations. The purpose of appraisal has been viewed in many different ways by many people. It has, for example, been used as the annual excuse for raking over all the errors an employee is perceived to have made during the last twelve months. Many line managers still view it as an exercise that has to be done once a year because HRM says so. It is my own view that one of the biggest benefits from a participative appraisal system is the fact that it happens. The formal meeting between an employee and the boss to discuss forthcoming objectives, each other's role in them, and the development needs of the individual both short-term and careerwise, is crucial to the organisation and its employees. The role of HRM is that of process management, not of process owner. Traditional views of appraisal have always held that it should be separate from the process of salary review. Certainly it may not be the place to discuss salary formally, but in the light of the current popularity of performance-related pay it is hard to keep the two processes unrelated. With this in mind, appraisal of performance has to be undertaken in a fair way in order that it can reflect true individual performance. This chapter looks at a methodology that can be adopted for performance appraisal that will help make other decisions taken as a result of such performance appraisal fair and, as far as possible, equitable. Chapter 7 looks at the utilisation of competencies within the process.

Rating performance

This is an area that gives cause for concern among employees. 'How can I be sure that I have been fairly assessed?' 'How do I know that if I am awarded a C by one manager, another might not have given me a B?' These are typical questions asked by employees with regard to performance appraisal. In a system that has no defined parameters for evaluating performance they are valid concerns. Too many performance-rating systems still use rating scales that have subjective ratings and otherwise make no attempt to establish a measurable rating system. Systems that use ratings such as 'good', 'above average', 'satisfactory', 'below average', 'excellent' or 'unacceptable' without any associated descriptors are wholly subjective and deserve the criticism levelled against them.

The purpose of appraisal can be seen as to provide an opportunity to renegotiate the output requirement from the employee in line with the needs of the business, both short-term for the coming year and longer-term. In terms of performance measurement, it is the outputs of the employee that the appraiser is interested in. How these outputs are achieved is less important, provided that they are within the agreed and acceptable parameters and philosophies of the business. This concept is nothing new: it is management by objectives (MbO; Drucker, 1954), a philosophy that has endured through several decades of management science. It has been updated and refined, but essentially it is concerned with agreeing a set of accountabilities with an employee and then working with the employee to see that the accountabilities, which by their very nature are business priorities, are achieved. This fits with the traditional business approach to appraisal in which the process is cascaded down the organisation, ensuring that each level of the organisation can enable the level above to achieve its own objectives together with its own unique contribution to the accountabilities. At this stage it is accountable performance that is being appraised.

By identifying what it is that each person is accountable for achieving, and expressing this in measurable terms, it is possible to arrive at a fairer and more consistent way of measuring performance. Many readers will have attended management courses where objective-setting has been included in the programme. There are quite a few models for ensuring that accountabilities or objectives are measurable. One mnemonic for the process is to ensure that the objective is 'SMART' – Specific, Measurable, Agreed, Realistic, Timebound. If, at the time of agreeing objectives for the forthcoming period, each accountability upon which the employee will have his or her ultimate performance measured is 'SMART', then the eventual assessment of performance will be as objective as possible.

By following such an approach, fears regarding comparative fairness may be overcome: every employee who achieves all of the agreed objectives will be similarly rated. The effect of the downward cascade will, by and large, ensure comparative required effort from each employee. Utilising this approach we can begin to build up a database of performance that can be relied on to give reasonably robust information to assist HRM.

Previous chapters have outlined the features of a relational database and how tables can be linked to each other. How can this be utilised within the sphere of performance measurement? First we need to develop a meaningful assessment scale that can be easily stored and analysed by a RDBMS.

Statisticians often argue against using a rating scale of odd numbers on the basis that it leads an assessor towards the central tendency and thus distorts the outcome. However, on this occasion a five-point rating scale will be utilised because here it is genuinely appropriate to have a five-point rating scale clustered around a central rating. To understand this reasoning a brief explanation is needed. In order to survive, a business or organisation has to be relatively successful. It must, by definition, be composed of employees who are, by and large, fulfilling their job roles to a level of expectation that means that they are achieving their accountabilities. If this were not the case, the organisation would not be thriving. It could of course alternatively be that employees are asked to achieve objectives that do not enable the overall organisation to achieve its goals, or that its goals are insufficient to allow organisational survival. However, for the most part the basic assertion of success must be true: the majority of employees are achieving what is expected of them. This being the case, any rating scale would have to show this as well – and provide an opportunity to show those outside the norm, who are either overperforming or underperforming. A suitable scale might be:

A   Achieving more than the agreed level of performance in all agreed areas

B   Achieving more than the agreed level of performance in more than 50 per cent of agreed areas

C   Achieving the agreed level of performance in all agreed areas

D   Achieving more than 70 per cent* of the agreed level of performance in agreed areas

E   Achieving less than 70 per cent* of the agreed level of performance in agreed areas.

*This should be measured against 70 per cent of the number of agreed accountabilities and can be adjusted to individual schemes. For example: if an employee has six areas of agreed accountability, this 70 per cent could be 66 per cent or four out of six.

By adopting this approach, a distribution of performance should emerge that is similar to that illustrated in Figure 6.

The figure shows both a numerical scale and an alphabetical scale. It can be seen that the employee performance

Figure 6

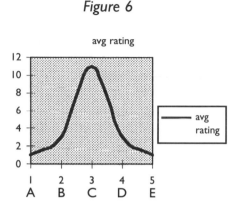

avg rating

clusters around the central tendency, and is thus representative of a normal distribution. A normal distribution would suggest that an organisation might expect to have about 70 per cent of its employees operating at an agreed performance level, approximately 12½ per cent operating at B and D respectively, and a further 2½ per cent operating at A and E. This is representative of reality. An organisation could not cope with more than the indicated levels of genuine high-fliers (where would they go?): more than this and it is predictable that some would soon be lost to the organisation. Similarly, more than this number of unacceptable performers would cause the organisation to suffer. It would also have to start looking at its recruitment systems. Categories B and D would be sustainable at the levels shown. B would represent the group of people likely to develop into jobs with greater responsibility, and the D group would be those who need to have more time spent with them to get them to achieve the required level. Employees at level C represent the core of the workforce. They are doing what is expected of them when it is expected, and are probably happy to continue to do so.

It is my personal view that this is the type of performance profile that organisations need in order to thrive and develop. Some organisations may wish to introduce more than five levels of assessment – perhaps seven – but it becomes more difficult to distinguish between bands the more bands there are. The relative measurements are sustainable within the measuring organisation, but they have no validity in cross-organisational comparisons. What is perceived as a required output level from an employee in one organisation may be very different in another organisation. In reality this is of no consequence, because an organisation is usually interested in its own requirements and not in comparisons.

Some organisations may feel the need to introduce a measurement band that signifies that the person has not been in post for long enough to be appraised. This is feasible, but it should be kept as a separate rating rather than seen as a subset of D or E. Equally, it is possible to set all new employees or employees new to a post reduced but measurable objectives to achieve, in order that they should achieve some performance rating at the earliest anniversary of appraisal. The important thing is for the expectations to be realistic.

Assessing potential

A further useful assessment that can be made at appraisal time is that of assessing the potential of an employee to take on greater responsibility. This choice of phrase is deliberately used, rather than the concept of 'promotability'. By measuring in terms of capability to take on further responsibility, an understanding could be made with an employee without alluding to some future promotion. If a rating was established as a level at which an employee would be promotable in the next 12 months, that would naturally become the expectation of the employee. All would be well if it happened. But, suppose that the promotion did not materialise. It is likely that a good employee, previously performing well, would become more and more disillusioned and demotivated as time went by. In the current climate of organisational delayering, consistent promotion can no longer be assumed by managers. It is far more common for employees to be moved sideways or to have their current jobs enlarged. To adopt the term 'capable of taking on greater responsibility' is to be no more than realistic that this will be possible. It does not guarantee to promote the person, and it will meanwhile be comparatively easy to find a way to enlarge his or her responsibility.

In establishing a scale for assessing potential, a similar argument would prevail as did in relation to the scale for appraising performance – except that assessing potential is more subjective. Best practice would suggest that such an assessment should arise from a discussion between manager and subordinate, which would lead on to an open assessment. It should be remembered that Data Protection legislation entitles an employee to see what data is held about him or her anyway, so there is little point in undertaking a covert assessment. The discussion may not be palatable to some employees, but it is important that an employee understands how he or she is viewed and has the opportunity to influence the decision either by discussion or by promised future action. The scale for a potential rating could also be a five-point scale:

A   Capable of taking on extra responsibility immediately or within 12 months
B   Expected to be capable of taking on greater responsibility after 12 months
C   Operating at the right level to match current abilities
D   Expected to be able to grow into current responsibility level within 12 months
E   Overstretched at current level of responsibility.

It is expected that an organisation would display a similar profile of potential as that shown in Figure 6 for performance assessment. Most staff would be operating at a 'C' rating. But in this case the proportion of people with the rating 'A' might be higher, with a corresponding drop in the group rating 'B'.

Inputting the performance data and the potential data into a RDBMS, it would be possible to plot the data on a graph. Whatever the shape of the graph, there will be messages for the organisation.

Using the computer in appraisal

All that has been said so far in this chapter can be applied to the appraisal of performance irrespective of whether the process involves the use of a RDBMS or not. The purpose of storing data on a computer is to enhance the process and to produce information to assist in managing the business. By adding a small data table to the existing database, a great deal

Table 23

APPRAISAL TABLE
EMPLOYEE NUMBER
DATE OF APPRAISAL
PERFORMANCE RATING
POTENTIAL RATING
APPRAISERS EMPLOYEE NUMBER

of management information can be produced. The data fields that are required are shown in Table 23.

Even with this small amount of data a number of useful management reports and profiles can be developed. It has already been suggested that for many organisations the graph shape for performance and potential will approximate to what is called the normal distribution. This can only be the case, however, if the organisation has been honest with its appraisal in the past, and if the organisation is successful and fully utilising the skills of its employees. An organisation that has not monitored its assessment processes in the past, perhaps because it has had no computer, and in which performance has not been measured objectively, will find that its graph shape is skewed.

There is a trend for employees to expect an 'A' rating for doing their job because this is perceived as being best. The assessment rating scale outlined here assumes that by being good at what he or she does and working to the expected level, a person's performance would be assessed as a 'C' – which is perceived by many as being third-rate. In this model it is not the case. Yet what tends to happen without clearly defined assessment criteria is a drift upwards toward 'B' and 'A' with no justification. Without a system of performance measurement management such as the one outlined here, therefore, an organisation can be skewed towards the upper ratings (suggesting an organisation composed of overachieving performers) when in fact the organisational performance is, with luck, achieving only the performance requirements to hit its targets. If pay is in some way linked to performance, a profile of this nature would mean that employees were getting paid for achievements that they were not making. This simple analysis can show that an organisation is not rewarding itself appropriately, in either direction. Why pay employees extra for doing what they are employed to do in the first place, just because it is more comfortable to award a 'B' at appraisal time? It is appreciated that this is an oversimplification of the reward systems in many organisations, but the point is well made. It may of course be that individual sections of the organisation stand out by not following the pattern set by the rest of the organisation. This information can lead to a further analysis of the department to assess the reason. Perhaps one department has a genuine difference in its general level of ability. It will need to be addressed, whether it leads to under- or overperformance. The former will slow down the rest of the organisation, and the latter will lead probably to frustration and possibly to unwanted staff turnover.

Superimposing the performance assessment graph onto the potential graph, it might be expected that both would roughly coincide. If that is not the case, then again it is an indication of a problem in the organisation. It may be a problem of accuracy of assessment, or it may show instead that the organisation is operating at the full potential of its current staff. If that is the case, there is an urgent need to inject people with vision and growth ability into the organisation.

The biggest benefit of storing such data as contained in Table 23 will come as a history builds up. Assuming that the data entered has been accurately assessed, it is possible through time to spot trends. It is unlikely that there should be any great difference between overall performances and potential year on year. If a sudden change does occur, it will need investigation. Similarly, an individual employee's performance or potential will probably not change dramatically year on year, particularly if he or she is still in the same post. It is a simple matter to devise a report that will show a listing of all employees who have a performance rating lower or higher than the previous year, who are still in the same job, and who have been appraised by the same manager. The same report could be produced for employees appraised by a different manager, and again for staff who now have different jobs. In fact, the query could be raised for any meaningful set of circumstances that was perceived to be useful. The reports could be generated by location or by department or even by individual appraising manager. This is all useful and often unused information by which to assess the effectiveness and fairness of application of the appraisal system.

Table 24 shows a table of ratings given by a manager to the staff that the manager has appraised. In a tabular form it does not appear to be a cause for concern. However, from the same data in Figure 7 a different story can be seen to be emerging. Representing information as a graph is a simple process for a RDBMS: it is a powerful way to spot different trends.

The graph shows that manager Y clearly has a tendency to assess employees more severely than the organisational average. This gives us information and reason to look further at the manager and assess whether Y is being fair. This can be achieved by looking at the performance of the sphere of operations within the business that the manager manages. If it is achieving its objectives, it is an indication that there is a need to tackle the harsh performance ratings. These figures may have developed over a number of appraisal rounds. If the department has been underperforming, then perhaps the information needs to be viewed in conjunction with that of manager Y's own boss. The reasons for the anomaly could be many and various. The point is that by storing this easy-to-enter data a great deal of information can be distilled. And by linking appraisal data to other data fields – such as ethnic origin, employee gender, employee grade – reports could easily be generated to ensure that individual groups were not being discriminated against. There should be no reason to suppose

Table 24

frequency	avg rating	manager Y
a=1	1	0
b=2	3	1
c=3	11	8
d=4	3	10
e=5	1	0
n	19	19
avge	3.8	3.8
stdev	4.147288	4.816638

Figure 7

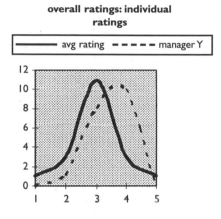

overall ratings: individual ratings

that any group, whatever its characteristics, should, on average, show any profile different from that of the organisation in general. Just because a person may have a low job grade in the organisational context does not mean that he or she should not be expected to perform at the 'C' level.

Building database queries

Until now this chapter has been concerned with showing organisational trends, trends that are indeed valuable as a way of monitoring the whole organisation and for producing reports. Useful reports can also be produced that are more individualised. A system like the one described in this chapter was implemented into a large organisation at the beginning of the introduction of low-cost computer technology to industry. This system enabled links to be drawn across data that had not been possible in the past. In the data table fields suggested for this chapter, the appraising manager's employee number was included. This provides the facility to link back to the details of the appraising manager's performance and potential details at the same time as those same details of the employees appraised by the manager. This can be a powerful tool – as the example below shows.

It is an easy task to set up a database query that will, from the data stored, produce a report of the performances and potentials of every employee. This may be very useful at times, but will require a great deal of scrutiny to get any useful management information from it. Computers are good at sorting and reporting data; humans are good at setting and solving problems by seeking specific information. What often prevents a problem from being investigated is the inordinate amount of time that it would take a human to categorise and sort all of the data. This is the strength of the computer – so let it do it.

Looking back, Table 23 shows the data held on each employee. By linking this to other tables described in Chapter 2, attached details such as department, location and employee name can be added. Department figures can be summarised and statistical reports can be produced that display the totals and averages of departments without identifying individuals.

In addition to these features a database has an ability to seemingly loop back on itself. What I mean by this is best explained by what is in fact a very powerful and useful example: a report that shows a listing of all employees who have a performance rating and/or potential rating assessed at a higher level than that of their boss. (It is assumed in this example that the appraising manager is the employees' organisational boss.)

Inputting a query to do this will change depending on the RDBMS host, but in principle it will be carried out as outlined below. It is effectively two queries in one: a powerful RDBMS allows a user to open the same table twice in the same query.

Figure 8 shows how such a query might be structured. The top part of the illustration shows how the links have to be made across the data tables. Notice that both the details table and the appraisal table are open twice in the query, once for each employee in the query relationship.

The arrows show how the first two columns are linked via the employee number to give details of an individual and his or her performance and potential ratings. The cross link occurs in row five, where it can be seen that the link is via the appraising manager's employee number: it was entered into the system via the appraisal form. This link to the second performance table and then to the second details table enables

Figure 8

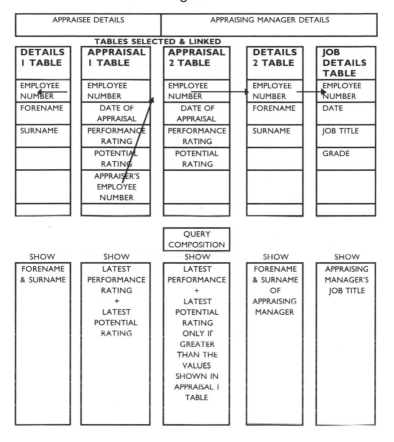

| APPRAISEE DETAILS | | APPRAISING MANAGER DETAILS | | |

TABLES SELECTED & LINKED

DETAILS 1 TABLE	APPRAISAL 1 TABLE	APPRAISAL 2 TABLE	DETAILS 2 TABLE	JOB DETAILS TABLE
EMPLOYEE NUMBER	EMPLOYEE NUMBER	EMPLOYEE NUMBER	EMPLOYEE NUMBER	EMPLOYEE NUMBER
FORENAME	DATE OF APPRAISAL	DATE OF APPRAISAL	FORENAME	DATE
SURNAME	PERFORMANCE RATING	PERFORMANCE RATING	SURNAME	JOB TITLE
	POTENTIAL RATING	POTENTIAL RATING		GRADE
	APPRAISER'S EMPLOYEE NUMBER			

QUERY COMPOSITION

SHOW	SHOW	SHOW	SHOW	SHOW
FORENAME & SURNAME	LATEST PERFORMANCE RATING + LATEST POTENTIAL RATING	LATEST PERFORMANCE + LATEST POTENTIAL RATING ONLY IF GREATER THAN THE VALUES SHOWN IN APPRAISAL 1 TABLE	FORENAME & SURNAME OF APPRAISING MANAGER	APPRAISING MANAGER'S JOB TITLE

The query will return only the records that fulfil the parameters defined in column three of the query.

the parameters to be set in the actual query. The final table is a straightforward link to the appraising manager, to give his or her job title, just as a way of proving identification. Further links could be made to identify location and department. Indeed, the job details table includes the job grade, which could easily be listed if required. In fact, any subsequent report could be ordered in job grade sequence, thus showing high-level organisational results first.

Once the links have been established, the actual query can be constructed. The query should contain two qualificatory selectors: one obvious, and one less so. The first parameter to be set is that the query shows only records which fulfil the criteria. In the column that contains the data fields for performance rating and potential rating, therefore, we must establish a method of ensuring that only those we are interested in are selected. The actual method for achieving this will vary depending on the RDBMS in use, but in plain English what is required is to

> *display all records where the performance rating in Appraisal 1 Table is alphabetically less than in Appraisal 2 Table AND where the potential rating is also less in Appraisal 1 Table than in Appraisal 2 Table.*

Using the rating scales described earlier, this query will now show only the records of the employees who have been allocated better ratings than their appraising managers have been given on both ratings. Employees with only one rating greater than their appraising manager's will not be shown.

The other qualificatory selector that must be used is not as obvious and may take a minute or two to understand. Because the database is built up over a period of time – indeed, that the data is historical is one of the greatest benefits – there will be as many appraisal ratings and potential ratings on record as the number of times appraisal has taken place since the RDBMS was introduced. However, for the purposes of this particular report we are not interested in the historical data. What we want to compare are the most recent ratings. For this reason, each record of entry in the appraisal table has an entry date included. It is this date which allows us to retain the integrity of the data, and which together with the employee number enables the record to be unique. There will only be one entry for an employee in the appraisal table on any date. The ratings may or may not change, but the two fields make each record unique.

To ensure that the query compares only the data from the last appraisal it will also be necessary to enter a criterion against the date field in a query. The inclusion of the date field is assumed in the above example, but it would of course be necessary in practice. Different RDBMS shells use different techniques for achieving the comparison of the correct data. Some may include what is effectively a function that looks for the 'latest entry'; others may not be quite as user-friendly and require the user to enter a date range; others may use a 'max date' function. The latter illustrates what it is actually necessary to do. As was explained in an earlier chapter, the computer stores dates by allocating a unique day number to each date, based on a start date (generally the beginning of 1900). It therefore follows that the highest-numbered date held in a set of records for an employee must be the latest entry in respect of that person. The same point would need to be borne in mind in relation to the job table. We would be interested in the latest job and not in all of the jobs that the manager had ever held.

Deciding which reports

This exercise has not been undertaken purely as an illustration of the power of the computer: there is a legitimate HRM reason for running such a report. Such a circumstance as an employee's outperforming his or her appraising manager could in fact be perceived as an organisational blockage. Left unmanaged, a situation could arise in which the organisation might lose the better-performing subordinate as a result of frustration and failure to be able to achieve his or her potential. By producing such a report, HRM can point the situation out to the manager of the appraising manager and also be proactive in what decisions are made in respect of the situation. The generation of the report does not imply that action must be taken, but it does illustrate anomalies that might well have otherwise gone unnoticed.

By inputting the small amount of additional data into the appraisal table as has been suggested, a number of useful reports that can be produced will help in the management of the appraisal system and in the supply of management information. There is no point in trying to list all of the possible information although it may be useful to illustrate what can be achieved.

Linking the tables of employee details, job details and appraisal, it is easy to produce an employment history for each employee showing the jobs held, the job grade at the time, the performance and potential at each review logged during the time that the job was held. The report could, of course, be grouped by department or by location or by appraising manager. While this report may be useful to produce on an individual basis when considering personnel for moving to other positions, a complete report of the history of every employee would be less useful. What is more useful is an exception report of performance and/or potential to pick out employees who have either improved or worsened their ratings since their last appraisal – especially if the rating has altered in either direction by a factor of 2. Information reported in this way is no hardship for the computer to produce but of considerable use to the manager. A further adaptation could be to produce a report grouped by each appraising manager. If the assessed performance of a group of employees has changed in either direction between appraisals, it may well be an indication of the appraisal skills of the manager or his or her approach to assessment. It could also be an indicator of workload as a result of changes made within the business since the last assessment round. Many organisations have downsized in recent years, and many employees report that they feel overwhelmed by the job requirements now placed on them. One indicator that might help an organisation to recognise this is the history of work performance. There are of course other indicators that are available on analysis of the HRIS database, notably labour turnover and absenteeism. An analysis of all such indicators is worth while as a way of helping to prevent the loss of valuable staff, who are even more crucial following any form of rationalisation activity.

The level of sophistication in reporting can be determined by the system user; the capabilities of the system depend on the amount of data stored in the first place. The skill of extracting information is as much a conceptual process as it is a technical process. And whether an organisation discriminates unfairly can be monitored easily by a RDBMS. A current HRM phenomenon is the 'glass ceiling'. By setting up the system to produce a report analysing career history and including the gender data from the employee details table, an analysis of actual behaviour can take place. The report can be a simple analysis of career progression and performance assessment against gender or ethnic origin, or it can analyse the percentage of each identifiable group in the workplace and compare each against the percentage of different groups, identifying ratings, job moves or promotions outside the organisational norms. Such reports can be grouped by department, by location or even by manager. Although the report may take a little time to set up on the system in the first place, like all reports it can be run at any time on the touch of a button. Similarly, the data can be extracted from the system and further analysed via a spreadsheet package. This is often easier for many users because they are more familiar with spreadsheets than with a database package. Generally, spreadsheets are less precise in the instructions that they require from the user. By producing reports such as the equal opportunities report outlined here, the system can produce factual evidence upon which a competent person may analyse the company's performance rather than rely on hearsay evidence and impressions. Such information may save an organisation a substantial amount of time and money, especially in situations where employees may be claiming that there has been some form of discrimination.

Appraisal management

A criticism often levelled at HRM concerns an apparent inability to manage the appraisal system. This may or may not be fair. Line managers in many organisations do not see the appraisal system as much more than an HRM requirement and are subsequently quick to criticise. The actual administration of the system, and to some extent the form-filling part, can be enhanced by utilising the HRIS system. Most organisations carry out appraisals once a year, some less often – but whichever, the gap tends to be constant throughout the organisation. The HRIS can again produce a report that highlights all employees who have not had the details of their latest appraisal entered within a predetermined period of time. It is a case of composing a simple database query that links the employee details table, the appraisal table and the job details table. From these tables the employee name, employee number, last appraisal date, job title, department and location can be identified, together with the details of the last appraising manager. By setting a condition on the 'appraisal date' data field that asks the system to return the details of any employee whose last appraisal entry date is less than 'Today – 395' and where 'date left' is blank, only records with a last entry date more than 13 months prior to the date of the report being run will be shown. This duration can of course be altered to suit the needs of the organisation. Whatever the duration specified, the report allows the HRM department to manage the process and to ensure that the data held is as up to date as possible.

It is also an easy task for the computer to produce individual appraisal forms for each employee, thus freeing a manager from having to fill in the biographical data in each form. It can also insert job title details, length of service, length of time in current job, a history of previous ratings, and details of whom the employee reports to and who is anticipated to appraise him or her. All that is required of the appraising manager is to amend any of the data that has changed from that which is held in the system. Of course, the rest of the document will have to be completed by the manager and employee in the usual way, but at least the data that could be expected to be already known to the organisation does not need to be repeated. In addition to the performance and potential ratings, there is much more to discuss at appraisal – much of which would not be worth entering onto a database. Avoid giving in to the temptation to store too much data with which little or nothing can be achieved. There is no point in storing data electronically if it can not be used to provide meaningful information.

One aspect that is growing within appraisal is that of job competencies. It is worth looking at it in some detail – and it is covered in the next chapter.

The individual appraisal forms, together with a report listing appraisees to be appraised by each individual manager, can be produced by the system and sent to the department head for distribution. It should be borne in mind at all times that such forms contain confidential information and must be treated with care.

7

MANAGING JOB AND MANAGERIAL COMPETENCIES

In addition to the ratings for performance and potential outlined in the previous chapter, the concept of competencies and their measurement can add much to the effective managing of the human resource within an organisation. The potential problem is deciding what to measure and what to store about individuals. To resolve this question let us think about the purpose for which we are seeking information about the individual employee. In the case of storing the data on an HRIS database, it is likely that the reason is connected to undertaking recruitment, succession-planning and employee development in relation to a set of recognised organisational competencies. For most organisations it is not worth setting up the system to be able to cope with all competencies developed for all jobs in line with those identified by the lead body for each job or group of jobs. This is not to denigrate the work done by lead bodies, but it must be recognised that the comprehensive range of competencies is generic and intended for indivduals as a development programme often linked to NVQs. True, an effective employee ought to be able to undertake the majority of the tasks within the set of competencies – but to ask a manager (and employee) to rate the employee annually against a full set of competencies would be unrealistic. A meaningful alternative has to be found.

Deciding what to measure

There are at least two approaches that can be used to resolve the problem of deciding what to measure and what to store. The information used in both approaches needs to be prioritised in a way that allows a business to identify what it is that makes an employee successful within the organisation. The difference between the two ways is in the perception of what a competence is. It may be that the reader will feel that the categories proposed for each approach could be applied within the same business but at different levels.

The first approach to the identification of job competencies utilises the types of categories that are familiar to most managers from the work done by lead bodies. These include such items as interviewing, counselling, holding meetings, setting objectives, communicating and interpreting organisational goals, achieving agreed goals, and financial awareness. The list can be as long as the number of skills involved in managing a business, but does not include individual job-related skills that might be expected in specific areas such as finance, research and development, and computer programming. If these are important to the progression of the employee through the business, or as a way of identifying successors, they could additionally be considered core competencies and recorded as such. The alternative approach to identifying job competencies – indeed, it may be seen as a complimentary approach by many – is to address the subject by looking at a more conceptual or abstract set of competencies – for example, the ability of an employee to identify and set long-term goals for an organisation, to analyse and diagnose a situation, to lead a group to a solution, to develop long-, medium- and short-term action plans in line with goals, to be self-controlled, flexible in method and focused in objective, to be aware of others' needs, and to be proactive.

The second approach may perhaps be regarded as an additional set of competencies that are applicable to more senior managers. Managers operating at a non-strategic level may not need to possess some of the abilities described here, whereas really senior managers may be beyond the need to have such skills as running meetings included in the regular appraisal of their competencies. Shortcomings in these areas could be highlighted by exception.

Whichever method or combination of methods an organisation chooses to take, it will be apparent that in order to manage the data in an effective way a systematic approach has to be undertaken. Many organisations, as suggested earlier, identify the 10 or 12 core aspects of being a manager or employee that generally lead also to being effective and successful within the business. This exercise can be achieved by setting up focus groups and asking managers what it is that they value most in their own performance and in the performance of their managers and their subordinates. Having undertaken this exercise, a set of realistic organisational core competencies can be listed.

Individual job competencies

It is possible to identify individual job competencies for each job. A computer can provide an organisation with a data table listing all of the competencies of each important job within the organisation. The table would start with the competency name and a unique code for each competence; a job analyst, together with the job holder or holders and managers, would then identify the most important competencies for each job and enter the codes into the individual job table. This would definitely tailor the competencies to each job or job group. It is certainly feasible to adopt this approach if the organisation wishes to invest so much time in the process. There can be no hard and fast rule about it. One major drawback in adopting this approach, however, centres on the rapidity of organisational change. Despite the time spent analysing and identifying the individual competencies of each job, it may well be that within a short space of time the particular job no longer exists.

It may instead be more sensible to adopt a mid-path through the two approaches. An organisation could identify perhaps 20 core competencies for the achievement of individual and organisational effectiveness. From these 20 an employee and the manager would identify the 10 most important competencies for the job that the employee holds. Not the ten that the employee is best at. Much the same method that was outlined in the last chapter to produce individual appraisal forms could be used again here to produce an individual list of competencies for the employee. Indeed, these could be included as part of the appraisal form.

The challenge in this exercise is to enter the individual job competencies into the system. There are a number of ways that it can be done, and it is worth spending a little time exploring those possibilities while also taking the opportunity to explore the concept of 'Look up' tables. The most important thing about the data entry to be used as a basis for comparison is consistency of entry. If an entry is typed differently, is wrongly spelt, or has an extra space in it, the computer will perceive the entry as different from other similar entries. Clearly, this is no use to us when we are seeking to analyse or group data. With something as complex as the logging of text entries to identify individual competencies it is almost inevitable that some typing errors will occur. But there is an easier way. The example below shows how selecting 10 from 20 competencies, as briefly discussed above, could be practically undertaken on a RDBMS. It is the concept of

Table 25
KEY COMPETENCY TABLE

COMP_NUM.	COMPETENCY
1	FINANCIAL UNDERSTANDING AND ABILITY
2	OBJECTIVE IDENTIFICATION
3	OBJECTIVE-SETTING
4	LEADING TEAMS
5	CUSTOMER CARE
6	MOTIVATING INDIVIDUALS
7	COUNSELLING
8	APPRAISING PERFORMANCE HONESTLY
9	SHORT-TERM OPERATIONAL PLANNING
10	LONG-TERM OPERATIONAL PLANNING
11	ACHIEVING ORGANISATIONAL GOALS
12	INFLUENCING THE ORGANISATION
13	CONTROLLING MEETINGS
14	PRIORITISING TASKS
15	GIVING INDIVIDUAL FEEDBACK TO OTHERS
16	TAKING FEEDBACK FROM OTHERS
17	BEING SELF-CONTROLLED
18	TECHNICAL ABILITY FOR THE JOB
19	ACTION TO CONTINUOUSLY SELF-DEVELOP
20	ABILITY TO UTILISE INFORMATION TECHNOLOGY WITHIN JOB

linking tables, or objects, that helps us to ensure consistency of entry into the system. By setting up a data table with the 20 competencies in it, and numbering each one, it is necessary for the text of the competencies to be entered only once. This largely overcomes the risk of error on entry and precludes most of the input operators' groans about volume of entry. When this table has been set up, other tables can be related to it to get the textual data that the human reader needs to make sense of the whole situation. The computer is quite happy to use the competency identity numbers. Table 25 shows an example of how such a table might be constructed – a simple table, but one key to the process of managing competencies within the organisation.

This table can be used as a basis for identifying individual competencies and job competencies. The list of competencies is not intended to be a definitive list: the competencies are very different from those that might be found in a set of competencies compiled by a lead body for a particular job. It is a list of competencies, or management skills, that an organisation might find are the ones displayed by its most successful staff.

The list probably represents too many competencies to be associated with any individual job. Indeed, some of the categories may not be applicable to certain levels of job. To identify the ten most important competencies in relation to each job is a simple matter of discussion between boss and subordinate which could be held either before or during appraisal.

Figure 9
JOB COMPETENCY TABLE

DATA FIELDS	DATA ENTRY AREA	
DATE		ENTER THE COMPETENCY NUMBER IN THIS DATA FIELD
JOB_NUM		
COMP1		
COMP2		
COMP3		
COMP4		
COMP5		
COMP6		
COMP7		
COMP8		
COMP9		
COMP10		

It might well be better to conduct the exercise at a separate time because it would probably otherwise make the appraisal meeting too long. To complete the exercise it will be necessary to produce an input document in hard copy which can either be entered into the system by hand, or – in a large organisation with many employees and jobs – be scanned into the system, thus alleviating input operator time. It is also likely that a brief explanation of the meaning of each of the competencies ought to be included in order to dispel any ambiguity of interpretation: the definitions could be agreed by a representative group of employees within the organisation. The computer would then build up a database table for all jobs, identifying a competence profile for each. Figure 9 (page 21) shows a table layout.

This layout also allows for the ten competencies to be prioritised in order of importance to any particular job. It might be difficult to achieve for all ten, and the result may well be regarded as subjective, but the exercise should at least identify the three or four most important competencies accurately. Those ranking lower will be less important anyway. The exercise will be of great value when the organisation is undertaking succession-planning.

So far I have described how to identify and record the 20 core competencies for success within an organisation, and described a process of aligning the ten most important of them to each job within the organisation. Even though an organisation may change its structure, this information may still be useful within the new structure. Data on a job level within the old organisational format can be associated with the new equivalent job level of the restructured organisation, and so constitute eminently usable information.

The next step in the evaluation of competence is to find a way to objectively and usefully assess an individual against the competencies identified for success within the organisation. The approach adopted within the NVQ-type approach is probably not sufficient in the case of assessing employees in an organisation. It is only necessary for an assessor to identify whether an indvidual working towards an NVQ is competent or not yet competent: degrees of competence are not relevant to the exercise. In the context of an organisation's measuring an employee's competence within a known range of competencies, however, there are a number of benefits to be gained by identifying degrees of competence.

In common with other aspects of people assessment – namely, the entry of data and the manipulation of data – consistency is required. It is necessary to develop a scale of ratings that fairly represents the array of possible abilities within the competencies and that can be applied to the whole list. Furthermore, the scale of ratings needs to be meaningful and relevant to the organisation, and not just be a numerical scale of perhaps one to five without any associated definitions or comparisons.

A list of possible ratings and their definitions is presented below as an example. It is based on the ability of an individual to visibly measure up to the identified competencies. It is therefore a physical and statistical measurement rather than a subjective opinion. The identified competencies have a behavioural (rather than cognitive) element to them that can be observed. But this does not mean, of course, that manager and appraisee will necessarily agree.

Possible competence ratings

1   No ability in this competency
2   Able to undertake this competency under supervision
3   Able to undertake this competency without supervision
4   Able to assist or supervise peer-group members to undertake this competency.

The number of competencies that an individual is measured against can vary. He or she might be measured against the ten identified competencies for the current job or, as may be more useful, against all of the identified criteria. This is a matter of organisational preference. But in terms of computer input requirements, it is only a question of entering a number against a data field. To achieve the technical input, all that is required is for a data table to be set up called 'Employee competence'. As in Figure 9 it would need a date field to be able to identify the annual entries. It would also need a data field to identify the employee (this would be the employee number). The number of competency fields would depend on the approach adopted, but if the employee was being rated against *all* of the identified competencies, that would mean a total of 20 data fields designated 'comp_num' (as in the key competency table) and another field called 'comp_level'. Each comp_num field would be linked to the same-named field in the key competency table for reporting purposes, thus identifying the name of the competency in that table with the level of competence in the current table.

This may sound like a lot of data to gather and enter – but if an organisation is going to reap the benefits of utilising the competency approach, then it is well worth while. The topic areas would be discussed at appraisal and career review time anyway. What this system is doing is placing a structure on the process. By utilising a checklist approach, all the manager and subordinate need to do is to agree a rating for each competency area. It is an opportunity to discuss the ways available to develop the areas of ability most needed by the company. It can also assist the training and development manager to focus development on the identified areas of need. Technically, all that is required is the formulation of an input screen that asks the operator to input the date, the employee number, and a value for each competency. Alternatively, documents could be scanned into the system.

Benefits to the organisation

There are many benefits to the organisation in carrying out the identification of core organisational competencies as outlined in this short but important chapter. The actual process of identification is probably the greatest single advantage of the exercise because it makes the organisation look at itself in a way that it may not have done before, and produces a profile of what a successful employee has to be able to do within the organisation. Such a profile should impact on the recruitment of new employees to the organisation and enable the recruiting managers to focus their selection on the things that truly matter to the organisation. If the organisation uses assessment centres or similar tools when recruiting, the identification of the competencies should strongly influence the format of any assessment carried out during recruitment. Exercises, case studies, role plays and psychometric instruments can be developed or used that afford an insight into a candidate's acquaintance with the prioritised competencies identified for the vacant position.

The data collected will be of use to the organisation when it is undertaking a skills audit and when formulating training and development plans. The data stored will produce a skills gap analysis profile for any employee. It is a simple matter to set up a report that will show the competency profile required for a job against the competency level identified for the job holder or proposed holder within those competencies. The report could display the numerical values of competence held by the individual and/or the textual definitions. The information could also be shown graphically: a horizontal bar chart is often a good way of displaying such data.

Clearly, one major use of such data would be in succession-planning within the organisation. The next chapter will explore succession-planning in greater depth but it is evident that from the data built up from the competencies it should be possible to produce reports that match the profile of an employee against the requirements of any job in the organisation, and that point out those employees who have a managerial profile that would be useful for the job. It does not, at this stage, distinguish between departments or between professional and craft skills; more of that later.

This chapter has confined itself to looking at managerial competencies and the part that they play in organisational effectiveness. The methodology described in this chapter could equally be applied within an organisation that wished to formulate employee profiles around professional or craft skills. It is unlikely that one table for competence would suffice, but it is likely that a table for each major skill or professional area could be developed. The data stored in such tables together with the organisational effectiveness competencies discussed in this chapter would give an organisation a very powerful database with which to help it make decisions. The downside, of course, would be the time involved in collecting and entering the data. Only individual organisations can make decisions on whether the process is viable for them. Such in-depth data collection and storage would probably be worthwhile to large, multisited organisations. Nevertheless, the watchword should be to store only the data that is going to be used effectively and that is going to enhance organisational performance to an extent greater than it costs the organisation to collect and store it.

8

BUSINESS AND SUCCESSION-PLANNING: THE ROLE OF HRM

There are a number of approaches to succession-planning that can be utilised by an organisation, ranging from a long-term strategic planning exercise to a short-term exercise identifying successors to current jobs within the organisation. This chapter looks at both approaches and discusses the techniques that might be used to achieve a required organisational outcome. The techniques involve management processes as well as technological processes. The rationale behind the use of technology is that it should represent an aid to management decision-making rather than a tool to carry out the decisions of management.

Strategic succession and HRM-planning

If HRM is to play the strategic role that it is capable of in an organisation, it has to develop reliable tools that can help it give high-quality input into decision-making at a strategic level. At the strategic planning stage a business is looking ahead for probably five years, and in some cases longer. Organisations have been criticised in the past for basing such long-term decisions purely on financial returns. The astute chief executive will have recognised the need to ground such decisions on a broader foundation of organisational factors affecting such long-term decisions.

Among these factors is the profile of staff required to enable the organisation to achieve its long-term goals. A major manufacturing organisation of a complex product, such as a car, will need to look at all aspects of its business before committing itself to long-term investment. The skills requirement of an organisation that plans to move towards the utilisation of electronic components within what has traditionally been a mechanical process will need to be carefully analysed. Major motor manufacturers have faced this challenge, among many others, over the last few years. The resultant change has had sweeping effects on the skills mix requirement of the organisations and their staffs, not only at the manufacturing stage but also within after-sales and customer care. Traditional motor mechanic skills have had to be enhanced in order that the company retains and develops its reputation and product reliability. At the earliest stages of the planning for such changes HRM needs to be involved. Indeed, at times it may well be that an organisation decides not to make a particular improved product on the basis that it does not believe that it could viably develop or attract staff to be able to manufacture the suggested product economically.

In any event, in order to be able to add to, and influence, such decision-making processes in an organisation, the HRM specialist will need sound information. Much of the data that has so far been collected will be invaluable to the organisation. In the example used above there is one large omission. What is the skills mix of the non-managerial workforce? In order to contribute to the decision-making processes HRM must surely have access to such information. Traditionally, appraisal has been seen as a process that does not include production workers or skilled non-managerial craft employees. But it can clearly be seen that in circumstances that require effective long-term people planning, for instance, a profile of skills mix and employee new skills trainability is important. The methodology for undertaking such an audit has already been outlined in Chapter 7, and although it was applied there to management and supervisory skills it can readily be adapted for non-management groups. It is likely that such a database would only be worthwhile to a larger organisation –

but how else could an organisation with several thousand employees manufacturing a complete entity such as a car keep track of its skills and successfully implement its development? How could such a database be designed and managed in a way that allows it to be kept as simple as possible but enables it to give as much information as possible? There is no simple answer to this question. One suggestion is that the problem should be addressed in a similar way to the competencies approach described in Chapter 7. Each major sector of the business should identify the key skills for its area of work, which should also include the key skills determined for the foreseeable future. A set of competencies would thus be developed for the body panel assembly plant, the paint shop, the trim shop, the engine assembly line, etc. A rating scale could be utilised like that in Chapter 7 with perhaps one further parameter: the ability to use this skill in other areas of the business. The ratings would therefore be:

1   no ability in this competency
2   ability to undertake this competency under supervision
3   ability to undertake this competency without supervision
4   ability to assist or supervise peer-group members to undertake this competency
5   ability to use this skill in other areas of the business.

The nature of the competencies would necessarily be skills-based and described as outputs rather than inputs. An example might therefore be: able to set up an engine to perform to manufacturer's specification – not: can use an electronic tuning machine.

Setting up such a database may seem a daunting task to the reader, but much of the information will be available at a local level – perhaps not in a competence format, but probably adaptable. Such data will be invaluable when making long-term manufacturing decisions. Because of the nature of the RDBMS it will be necessary only to enter the specific data regarding the competencies, a date to allow the entry to become unique, and the employee number. This table of data can then be linked to all the other tables, thus allowing full analysis of the data. Figure 10 gives a graphic representation of

Figure 10
ENGINE SET-UP COMPETENCY

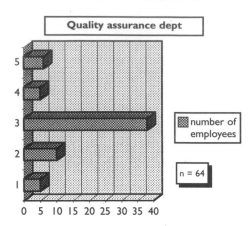

an analysis of the quality assurance department and the competency for engine set-up.

Information such as the summary of competencies can probably be best illustrated via a horizontal bar chart. The differentials between ratings are clearly emphasised. Figure 10 shows the data for one particular department, but it is just as easy to show the data for the whole company or to prepare an employee profile showing individual competencies. Such an analysis would allow an organisation to develop a skill mismatch profile and a subsequent development plan. To undertake this second stage of the process it is necessary to identify the optimum number of employees with a competency level of 3 or above. This may be as simple as identifying the number of work positions, adding an allowance for absenteeism, and multiplying by the number of shifts. A simple report can be prepared that subtracts actual from requirement and returns a numerical answer. A positive number reveals a shortage of skilled people against requirement; a negative number shows a skills surplus.

Within the long-term strategic planning exercise, the skills profile of the whole organisation would be matched against an estimated requirement of skills, and a subsequent mismatch profile would be developed. This could be presented both numerically and graphically.

Preparation of this strategic skills profile and analysis would probably be best effected by producing the actual skills analysis report within the RDBMS and then exporting the data to a spreadsheet package where a 'What if' or scenario-type analysis can be undertaken without having to set up formal reports and protocols.

The visibility of the data on a spreadsheet and its capacity for adding the proposed strategic requirement for each competence area, whether craft-based or management-based, makes the spreadsheet an easier tool to use for such tasks. It is also likely that managers will be more comfortable working on a spreadsheet than manipulating a database. Using the function and formula features of a spreadsheet allows a model to be built up by the manager that can not only analyse the skills gaps but also arrive at a costing of the whole exercise, which can be updated by adjusting just a few cells. Development and manipulation of spreadsheets in this way is further explored in a later chapter.

By including the individual skills of employees both in craft and in management skills within the RDBMS, the contribution of HRM within the strategic planning processes of the organisation can be greatly enhanced.

Because the database has been built up in an object-oriented fashion, and employee data is held in a linkable form throughout the RDBMS, skills analyses like the ones described can be extended to include employee date of birth as well as job title, job group, location and department. Age profiling is thus readily made possible, which would allow an organisation to see how the skills profile that it currently has will change over the next five to ten years as a result of retirements and predicted staff turnover by age groups. It is likely that younger employees will experience a turnover higher than employees aged over 40. To produce an age profile analysis by skill and by department manually would be an extremely difficult task, probably not even viable, but using the data held within the database it is a relatively easy analysis to undertake. It is a tool that certainly enhances the usefulness of HRM within the business. Like all reports set up within the system, it can be run as often as required once the initial report routine has been identified. Each time that the report is run it will automatically utilise the current data in the database, ensuring that the information given is the latest available and most up to date.

Every organisation will have its own view of what competencies it needs to measure and what aspects of its workforce are important in the long-term analysis of its employees. Few organisations will today have the same skills profile that they had ten years ago. The impact that technology and changing world markets have had will have led to a broader skills base in some ways, while in other areas it will have caused a de-skilling of jobs. If they have a database of organisational data such as has been described here available, organisations can rely on accurate information upon which to base their long-term human resource plans.

Succession-planning

Succession-planning lends itself to utilising the power of the computer. Sometimes seen as a controversial topic, it is still not undertaken by some organisations. Many would argue that the practice undermines the equal opportunities philosophy, but while this may be an interesting philosophical question, it is not one that will be debated to any great degree here. It may well be that if job vacancies were automatically filled by identified successors without the intervening process or advertising a vacancy, at least within the organisation, other employees would protest. However, succession-planning is not necessarily about slotting people into jobs; it is more about ensuring that there are sufficient people within the organisation to be able to cover key jobs within the business. This does not necessarily mean that a vacancy should not be advertised. It does mean that if succession-planning has been properly undertaken there should be people immediately available who can legitimately apply. If an organisation is applying a succession-planning model to its business, it could in fact mean that there are greater opportunities within the business for existing employees. A further criticism levelled against it, however, could be that by adopting this approach an organisation might become too inward-looking and lack the stimulus in terms of new ideas that candidates from outside the business bring. As long as an organisation is aware of the potential pitfalls of the systems that it operates, it will be able to keep a balanced view. No sensible organisation is likely to adopt just one single system of recruiting staff into jobs. The fact is that HRM in conjunction with other organisational managers, must seek to recruit the best person for the job. If that can be achieved from within the organisation and it is viewed as the right move, why on earth undertake expensive recruitment externally?

Much of the data that has already been entered into the database is of use in the succession-planning process. The process can be enhanced further by the addition of a number of extra data fields. These need to be explained, but together also demonstrate a model of succession-planning that could be simply adopted with only a little extra computer input. The approach described here takes the fundamental position that succession-planning is about identifying potential successors to a job or type of job. While it is inextricably linked to people, its purpose is not to plan individual careers. One of the consequences of succession-planning may well be to assist the development manager to bring about career-relevant development opportunities for individuals, but this is not its primary objective. The purpose of succession-planning, as described here, is to identify jobs that are at high risk in the organisation and, should they suddenly become vacant, to enable the organisation to manage the situation. One of the questions that might legitimately be raised concerns the dynamic nature of the organisation. What is the point of identifying successors to jobs that may not exist in the future, or which might change? This is a valid point, but not one that is considered forceful enough to obviate the need to be looking to the future. Indeed, succession-planning could be seen to enable such change. Except in the most extreme of examples the functions of most jobs continue to be necessary to an organisation even if the job itself changes direction or shape.

Additional data fields

As previously mentioned, a few new data fields are required to set up meaningful succession-planning. These fields could be added to the 'Job table' object, but for ease of identification and auditing it is probably best if a separate table called 'Succession' is developed. The new fields to enter will be job risk to the business, and probability of succession (successor1, lead_time_1, date_1), (successor2, lead_time_2, date_2), (successor3, lead_time_3, date_3). The link field will be the job number. Each of these extra fields will be explained, as will the methodology of the process. Briefly, what is described below is a computer-assisted process that involves an upward-cascading series of meetings within the organisation to discuss each job or group of jobs, with a view to identifying succession. Although data held about each job and the potential successors to it is used to aid decision-making, the method is not an automated process over which managers have no control. This will be expanded upon as the chapter proceeds.

Job risk to the business factor

There can be no argument that some jobs within an organisation are more critical than others. Most would agree that the managing director carries more responsibility than a shop floor production worker. For succession-planning, what we are concerned with is the risk to the business of a job's suddenly becoming vacant. It is the suddenness of this event that can cause problems within an organisation if it is ill-equipped to deal with the vacancy. If a key production worker does not arrive for work, it could mean that a whole shift might not be able to produce, all because of one break in the link. It is extremely unlikely that this would happen: most organisations have short-term contingency plans for such an eventuality. The fact is, though, that the immediate effect on a business is felt more on the absence of a supervisor or junior manager than on the absence of a senior manager. This is because, for the most part, supervisory and first line management are concerned with the problems of the current day and achieving the needs of the current day and/or the next few days. The contributions of the managers at higher levels are more medium- to long-term; they are often concerned with procedures and strategic issues – problems that have a longer-term impact. The job risk to the business rating is concerned with immediacy rather than with overall effect. It is true that the lack of strategic or longer-term management may eventually have a greater impact on the overall business than the loss of a supervisor, but there is more time to manage the situation than if a supervisor or more junior manager is lost. This method therefore proposes that each job should be rated against the following or similar scale:

1   An immediate effect will be felt by the business if this job is not filled
2   An effect will be felt by the business within two weeks if the job is not filled
3   An effect will be felt by the business within four weeks if the job is not filled
4   An effect will be felt by the business within 12 weeks if the job is not filled
5   An effect will be felt by the business within six months if the job is not filled.

Examples of jobs that might fit into these categories are:

1   a first line supervisor or key technician required to be operating at all times during a process
2   an office manager who has introduced systems into the department but without whose personal presence short cuts might be taken or outputs might not be forthcoming after one or two weeks
3   a quality assurance manager who has set up quality systems and enforced them, but without whose management the processes might start to deteriorate after four weeks
4   a departmental manager who has control of the medium- to long-term aspects of the business, but on whose absence the department would after 12 weeks or so start to underachieve because of a lack of focus on the wider business needs
5   an organisational head, after whose loss the whole business would start to lack dynamism and long-term planning, thus in six months or so losing its unique ability to influence the market and adapt to the market.

These examples are intended as illustrations rather than definitions. Organisations can use as many ratings as they see fit to, and classify them in any way. The feature of the data field is the fact that it is defined in an alpha/numerical sequence which will allow the computer to sort or filter the data in a meaningful way.

By entering this data for each job and linking across to the job table, we can quickly generate a report that can give us the risk rating of all of the identified jobs in the organisation by department, location and job title. Linking the query for this report still further to the employee details table, we can identify the current job holder of the job or, in the case of a blank entry in the job holder identity number field, the risk ratings of current jobs not filled. It is probably the latter information that an organisation would want to be able to generate quickly, for it would show where to concentrate recruitment effort.

A further report that might be useful to generate from the data so far entered would be a comparison of the grade of the job holder with the job risk factor. It is a reasonable assumption to make from the model suggested above that the higher the grade of a job, the lower the immediate risk to the business. I have myself encountered examples of where relatively senior management jobs were actually classified as high-risk solely because the job holder had not developed adequate protection systems for the organisation and in fact kept too much information in his or her head, thus putting the organisation at risk. Once this situation is identified, the organisation and HRM can start to build systems that protect the organisation.

One particular example involved a purchasing manager who had not set up a record system of contacts and product material sources. The situation was highlighted when all jobs were classified into their job risk categories. A database of contacts, etc, was subsequently developed, thus reducing the job risk component of that particular job.

It will be apparent that the process of identification of job risk cannot be undertaken in isolation; it has to be undertaken in conjunction with the department heads for the jobs being classified. It is the current risk to the organisation that is required. Only by asking what will actually happen if no one takes on the job can the risk be assessed. The model used here is strongly representative of a commercial organisation. Large non-commercial organisations, such as hospitals, may have senior members of staff who occupy jobs that genuinely expose the organisation to a high risk if they are not replaceable. For example: a consultant surgeon may well be classified as a category A risk.

The proposed methodology of the succession-planning process includes the suggestion that each department (or other convenient organisational demarcation) meets level by level to discuss the succession of the jobs in the tiers below them. The meetings would not start at a junior level but more likely at that of department manager. This level of managers could discuss all the jobs within their spheres of accountability and additionally make valid observations about other areas of the sector of the business that they work in, in that some staff may well formerly have reported to different managers. Figure 11 gives an illustration of the typical levels within a production department at which a succession-planning meeting might be carried out.

Figure 11

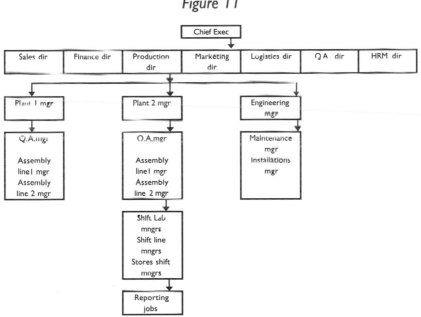

Succession probability

Succession probability is a useful item of data to enter into the succession data table. It is probably one of the most subjective pieces of data in the whole system, but it is nevertheless a useful factor to consider, comprising an estimate of the likelihood of a job's becoming vacant within the next 12-month period. As an estimate it would not be precise, but it is often the case that a manager knows when an employee is considering moving on or looking for a different position within the organisation. The rating can be categorised as a number between zero and nine, nine indicating a very high probability that the job will become vacant and zero the opposite.

Before dismissing the idea out of hand, it is worth thinking about it in more detail. The succession probability in relation to a job will not only be influenced by the intentions of the current employee, it will also be influenced by the organisation. In a case where an employee has been identified as ripe for a move to a different job, the rating will be a value at the higher end of the scale, depending on the certainty with which the move can be predicted. This statistic can then be added to the information about all of the jobs within the organisation that have a high job risk factor and which are likely to become vacant in the next 12 months. The resultant level of information enables the organisation to further refine its HRM efforts to ensure that, as far as possible, risks are covered.

Successor identification

At this point in the data entry it will be beneficial to have made use of all the other data that has been stored in the database to assist in identifying successors to actual jobs. The input data for this successor identification is clustered in three data fields: successor(n), lead_time_(n), date_(n). As shown earlier, there can be a number of these clusters. It is suggested that three clusters is as many as is practical for succession planning.

The successor(n) data field is intended to contain the employee number of the prime candidate for succession. The lead time(n) is a numerical value showing the number of months before the potential successor could take over the role. And finally, the date(n) is the date of data entry which is input in order to make the record unique and to be able to base calculations upon.

Clearly, to arrive at such data inputs it will be necessary to have access to individual competency levels and, where appropriate, professional or craft skill requirements for the job as well as those held by the successor under consideration. For high-risk jobs within an organisation it is probably best to be able to identify three successors.

At this time it becomes even more apparent that there is a huge payback to the organisation for taking the trouble to enter the data into the system. By querying the database it is now possible to identify potential successors to jobs by analysing their current capabilities in terms of the key organisational competencies. The reader will recollect that one of the ratings for the key competencies was an ability to supervise one's peers in undertaking the competencies. If this is the profile that an employee has, together with a performance rating less than or equal to C and a potential rating of B or A, then we can start to argue that this person has to be a potential successor to his or her organisational boss's job or a similar position. Indeed, with the data held we can confine our query to department or even job type, (ie supervisory, managerial, etc). The permutations are manifold; it is up to the reader to decide whether the query is giving useful information.

In an ideal world the HRM manager would control the process of the succession review meetings and would be able to access the database directly during the meeting. It would certainly be possible to set up the type of query and report that might be required in advance of the meeting, leaving the only entry requirement to be the parameters or data ranges of the query. A specific department can be quickly entered into a parameter statement that has an underlying query already defined. A query that perhaps raises data about all of the people within the organisation that have a particular competency at level 5 and who are at, or one below, the grade for a job that is being reviewed can also be prepared in advance, leaving the only input to be the grade level below which the information is needed. This type of query is commonly used in database interrogation. In the case of succession review and planning, much of the information that might be required during a meeting is predictable: it is just the groupings that need to be qualified further. Indeed, the same query might be asked several times during a meeting in relation to a different grade of job or a different department. As demonstrated in Chapter 2 it is a useful feature of a RDBMS that once a query has been devised and is yielding the information required, it is possible to save it so that the same question can be asked as many times thereafter as required. The query will usually return the information in a tabular form which is often sufficient, but – as seen previously – the information can be presented in report form, which again may be formatted in advance. From this, complex sequences of information can be grouped onto a report and further calculations can be made if necessary.

Table 26 shows an example of a report that could be generated before the annual succession review meeting is held. On an ongoing basis it will serve as an output report and as an input document. Initially the only data likely to be entered onto the form from the system would be the details about the job itself and the details of the current holder. This document would then be the basis for discussion at the succession review meetings, where potential successors could be identified and their details entered manually into the report for later inclusion into the RDBMS. An electronic input document on screen that is the same as Table 26 would be the easiest way for an operator to enter the data. Most of the data fields would be locked as display-only in this form because they are extracted from other tables within the database: it would upset the data integrity to alter data through this form. It is obvious that there would be no need to alter the job details or the details of the current job holder – these are all stored elsewhere. The data fields to be entered on this form, electronically, would be in the 'Possible successors' section. A valid employee number would have to be added to create the link to other data, and the operator should enter the lead time figure. Apart from that, all of the displayed information in this section is drawn from other areas of the database.

Table 26

	SUCCESSION REVIEW	PLANNING DOCUMENT		DATE PRINTED DD-MM-YYYY
JOB DETAILS				
	LOCATION		DEPARTMENT	
JOB GRADE.......				
JOB RISK		JOB TITLE		
SUCCESSION PROBABILITY	....			
TOP TEN JOB COMPETENCIES REQUIREMENT				
1	2	3	4	5
6	7	8	9	10
CURRENT HOLDER DETAILS				
NAME			EMPLOYEE NUM	
TIME IN COMPANY		TIME IN THIS JOB	AGE	
	PERFORMANCE RATING	POTENTIAL RATING		
THIS YEAR	....	....		
LAST YEAR	....	....		
PREVIOUS	....	....		
CURRENT	COMPETENCY	RATINGS		
1	2	3	4	5
6	7	8	9	10
11	12	13	14	15
16	17	18	19	20
POSSIBLE SUCCESSORS		CURRENT RATINGS	LEAD TIME TO SUCCEED	TIME IN PRESENT JOB
1 EMP NUM				
NAME		PERFORM..........	MONTHS............	MONTHS........
CURRENT JOB		POTENTIAL........		
CURRENT GRADE				
2 EMP NUM				
NAME		PERFORM..........	MONTHS............	MONTHS........
CURRENT JOB		POTENTIAL		
CURRENT GRADE				
3 EMP NUM				
NAME		PERFORM..........	MONTHS............	MONTHS........
CURRENT JOB		POTENTIAL........		
CURRENT GRADE				

After year one, the entries on the form would be complete and could be printed off ready for the next succession review. Most important is the ability to identify a successor or successors to all the jobs that the organisation wants to have a successor identified for. The information can be called up any time the organisation has a vacancy. This is a powerful tool for an HRM department to have at its disposal: it can help prevent poor appointments or poor promotions. The system will clearly show candidates who are not worthy of taking on a job of greater responsibility, and will help the department to over-come any 'halo-or-horns effect' resulting from inappropriate internal appointments if they do happen.

At this stage it is worth spending some time looking at some of the information contained on the succession-planning review document that has not been discussed up to this point: time in company, time in present job, lead time to succeed, and age. The last of these may well be viewed as a controversial com-ponent to include; it is nevertheless included in recognition of its possible usefulness as a component in the decision-making process. At present there is no legislation regarding age dis-crimination within the UK. Whatever the personal views of individuals, it is a fair component to add to a decision. Age is a factor that should be considered, but not one that should automatically exclude a candidate from consideration. There are many companies that prefer to attach a risk to a more mature member of staff, knowing that they are more likely to retain the person than they perhaps would a younger person. Equally, there are situations in which a person who is approach-ing retirement – even though he or she is just as likely to be per-forming at the required level as a younger person – may not be seeking further responsibility. There is no rule or average that can be applied: suffice to say that each case must be considered on all of its merits. It is my own belief that age is a factor that must be considered in a mature and professional way: any attempt to dismiss particular age groups without discussion must be avoided. It is part of the role of a mature HRM depart-ment to bring balance to this debate.

The time in present job information is less contentious than the age debate. It is generally acknowledged that there is a time lapse between promotions or after receiving greater responsi-bilities while the employee gets to grips with the new job skills and, perhaps more importantly, the new or wider sphere of influence that the job has. Similarly, if a person remains in a particular job role for, say, two years, then it may be that he or she will have achieved all of the possible development from the particular job, particularly if the situation is identified in con-junction with a performance level of B and a potential rating of B or A. This information is giving a good indication that the person is ready for a move or greater responsibility. A further look at the individual competencies should confirm this. Because there is a fair chance that such questions will be asked about potential successors at a succession review meeting, reports can be run off in advance identifying the potential and performance ratings, individual competencies and time in present job for all staff, or all staff who are performing at $< = B$ with a $< = B$ potential rating. These reports do not limit the succession to this group because managers at the meeting may introduce other candidates, but some reason would have to be given for why the newly proposed candidates did not get the higher ratings at review time and yet are being put forward for succession to a job. They could of course be identified as a third successor, with a lead time of perhaps 24 months.

This brings us on to the last of the data fields that is worthy of a brief explanation.

The lead time to succeed is an estimate of how many months it will be before the identified successor is ready to take on the position. The figure is best entered in months because that is more informative than 'less than 1 year', etc. It is worth entering all the time spans that relate to succession-planning in months.

The reader may be left with the impression that the succession-planning model put forward here requires successors to be identified for all jobs within an organisation. This, clearly, is not the case. There will be some jobs within any organisation that do not need successors – indeed, it might well be an unnecessary on-cost to establish them. There will also be jobs that will have to be directly recruited from the external labour market. It is likely that these will be the jobs with the most transferable skills, such as operative and clerical positions. Each organisation must make its own decisions with respect to its own needs. Do not conversely assume that the need for an identified successor is confined to the higher levels of an organisation. It may equally well be the case that for a highly specific and specialised position it may be uncco nomical to employ a person just to ensure succession. For example: an organisation may be large enough to have a safety officer, but rather than identify succession it may well decide to recruit from an external source, should the need arise. Whatever the organisation decides, the fact is that the contingency has been taken into account and the risk to the business has been assessed. The process of succession-planning has enabled the organisation to be as much in control as it could hope to be. This, surely, is a major benefit.

Data Protection

Although aspects of this topic were dealt with in an earlier chapter, it is worth spending a few minutes looking at it in relation to succession-planning.

The Data Protection Act 1984 is quite clear on the fact that an organisation must be registered to hold data on individuals, and that it must specify the purposes for which it holds data. Furthermore, and perhaps most importantly, it states that employees or data subjects are entitled to see exactly what is held on the electronic database that directly relates to them, whether fact or opinion. This is the case in law and, indeed, is only what most people would consider ethical. Little of what has been discussed in this chapter would be unknown to the employees anyway. If the organisation is practising open and honest appraisal and potential rating, the employees will know what is held about them. The Act does allow for non-disclosure of information where the release of the data is likely to be prejudicial to the organisation. In terms of succession- or career-planning it could be argued that to allow an employee to know that he or she is destined to succeed a certain person into a particular job could well be defined as prejudicial to the business. Succession-planning is not an exact science, and planned scenarios may not come about for a multitude of reasons. However, if an employee is under the impression that he or she is to succeed another person and it does not happen, he or she would most probably become demotivated and perhaps even leave the organisation. The disclosure of such information or associated information must therefore be prejudicial to the organisation.

Outputs of the succession review processes

Having collated all of this data about individuals, jobs and successors, how can HRM and other organisational managers use it to manage the business more effectively? Some of the reports that can be generated by the system as a result of the information held in the RDBMS supply the answer to this question. Each individual organisation will have things that it needs to discover about itself. The illustrations below are intended to act as a catalyst or stimulus to each organisation.

Simple listings

One of the most powerful tools that a computerised database can bring to data handling is its rapid ability to put data into a usable order or set of groupings. In a matter of seconds a database can be reordered and sequenced by any data field that the user requires, as long as it makes sense to sort on the field. In a simple listing of forename, surname, job title, department, location and start date we can both group the data in a variety of ways and order it in a variety of ways also. For example: with the data suggested here we can ask the database to group the data first by location, then by department, and then to show names in alphabetical order of surname and to include each employee's start date. Imagine how long it might take a clerical employee to undertake such an exercise for an organisation comprising a thousand people. The computer can do it in seconds – and, if the user then decided that the data should be grouped by employees' length of service, a small change in the query and the answer would be shown. This power is often underestimated. Most database systems allow the user to switch off repeating fields, so where the user is asking for information to be grouped by a location, although each record stores a location field, each grouping will be shown only once at the start of the group. The system will even know when printed output starts a new page, so that it will repeat the groupings at the top of each new page.

Useful Reports

Employees listed by location, department and age   To predict future recruitment requirements it is useful to have this type of analysis to hand. It may be useful to include a grouping by job title as well, particularly in a department where there are many jobs of a similar nature. An example of what such a report might illustrate to the organisational planners is that within a space of a five-year period all of the staff in the technical department are due to retire. Or it may show that this is not due to happen for another ten years or so, but it could be that this is the time to start planning how to maintain a seamless succession or recruitment.

Employees grouped by location, department, grade, gender and salary   Reports of this nature can be invaluable to an organisation in terms of monitoring its behaviour with regard to equal opportunities. With a little modification to the simple listing, the nature of such a report can be changed to show the variances of salaries of employees or groups of employees. Count the number of employees in various grade bands and compare them by percentage with the number of other groups. To expand on this point, it would be a simple matter for a report to count the number of male and female employees in an organisation and to compare the percentage of male managers to male employees and female managers to female employees.

In cases of dispute it would be possible to see if an organisation was in fact practising equal pay for equal value of work, although to achieve this the job grade would need to be included.

Current employees   It is easy to overlook the simplest of reports, but to produce a listing of all employees by location and job title can quickly be done. It can be further enhanced by grouping the report data by supervisor or manager, so listing groups of employees reporting to individual managers. This link would be made by including the data field of 'job reports to' from the jobs table and linking this back to the employee details table. Although the RDBMS is unlikely to be able to produce graphic organisation charts, this listing may act as a source for such charts to be prepared on a suitable graphics package. Microsoft Powerpoint will produce organisation charts, for example.

More specific reports
When the report outputs need to be more specific, the points made in the above examples hold good. But there are, of

course, particular circumstances in which additional information is useful.

Job risk 'A' or 'B' and no identified successor   An invaluable report for an organisational resourcing manager to possess, it can be recalculated at any time once a query is set up. The query has to be written in a way that covers all of the eventualities. To ensure that job risks of A and B are selected from the database, the query criterion in the job risk field needs to be < C (less than C). As far as the computer is concerned, it sorts alphabetically in 'ascending' order, and C is 'higher' than B and A. By including this criterion only the values of 'A' or 'B' are returned. To establish whether a successor has been identified or not is a little more complicated, and is wholly dependent on the way that data has been entered into the field. It is most important to set the field up in the database as requiring an input entry. If the entry is then left blank, the system will not allow the operator to proceed. Further to this, we can stipulate what the entry may be. In the case of the successor1 field, the input can be defined to comprise certain acceptable keywords or a number. Remember that identified successors were entered into the field by employee number and then linked to the details table to identify the name. The acceptable keywords would likely be 'none', 'external' or 'graduate entrant'. To find out which of the jobs selected from the first criterion in the job risk field also have no successor, it is therefore necessary to enter in the criterion for the successor1 data field 'none' or 'external' or 'graduate entrant'. In plain English, we are asking the database to select all records that are either 'A' or 'B' for job risk *and* have either 'none', 'external' or 'graduate entrant' entered into the successor1 field. We know that successor 1 cannot be blank, and we also know that if it has a number there is a successor, so by defining the criteria as such the required output must be achieved. It can also be understood that entries in successor2 field or successor3 will be there only if successor1 has a numerical value, so for this query we can ignore them. Table 27 shows how the query could be constructed in the database. From this it can be seen how important consistency of entry is. The application would reject misspellings, blanks and non-acceptable words.

Table 27

Job risk A or B	and No successors				
FIELD NAME	job risk	job title	dept	location	succession
CRITERIA	show data <C	show data	show data	show data	'none' OR 'external' OR 'graduate entrant' show data
GROUPING			GROUP BY 2	GROUP BY I	

Level 'A' performers with or without successors   The variety of reports that can be defined will reflect the importance to the organisation of the circumstances. There are many ways to present what is effectively the same source data but collated differently in order to answer specific questions.

In this example it is predicted that someone performing at an acknowledged level 'A' performance (exceeding all accountabilities of the job) is likely to be approaching the limits of his or her expectations of the job and be looking for the next challenge. Although there will probably only be approximately 3 per cent of the workforce in this position, it is essential that this small group is recognised and their careers managed. By producing the reports identifying the group of 'A' performers, we can do a number of things. We can consider their career development (the subject of the next chapter), and we can consider the risks to the organisation of their highly likely move. Bear in mind that the succession probability rating for such a group will be high as well. If we can further identify the job risk of this group, we can seek to minimise any predictable risk to the business from the employee moving into a new job. And, of course, having undertaken this exercise we will be more aware of the employees we risk losing if we cannot satisfy their aspirations.

Poor performers with or without identified successors   This query can be produced simply by changing the criterion in the 'level 'A' performers with or without successors' query to >C. This will then only select staff with performance ratings of D or E because these can be the only entries in the data field greater than C, and 'C' by definition is a person who is achieving all of the accountabilities of the job. The user can choose to distinguish further by selecting the succession criterion to be numerical to identify succession, or to enter 'none' or 'external' or 'graduate entrant' to establish that there is no identified successor.

To establish that there is a successor for a job is not as simple as entering that the value should be a number. What has to be entered is in fact a criterion statement that establishes that the entry in the field is 'not none', 'not external', 'not graduate entrant'. The word 'not' is known as a 'reserved' word in database query language, and should be used only to establish that one value is not equal to another value. This may seem convoluted, but since we know that any other value in the field must be a number, then by default if the value is not one of the three word strings it must be a number – and if it is a number it then identifies a successor.

In the last chapter we defined a report that listed all employees who were performing better than their organisational boss. With the information added to the database in this chapter we can now also establish whether the boss has an identified successor, whether it is the employee who is outperforming the boss, and also whether the employee himself or herself has an identified successor. This is a quality of management information that few HRM departments have had at their disposal in the past. It enables the organisation's managers to discuss deliberate succession moves and to ensure that the organisation seeks to keep the achievers. It attempts to place an objectivity on the process of appraisal and succession-planning that enhances the business in a way that would not be possible without the reporting and querying power of the computer. As we shall see in the next chapter, it can also allow us to channel our development efforts towards employees who will yield the best returns. Development funds spent on poor performers with little or no potential cannot be the best use of a scarce resource.

In conclusion to this chapter on succession-planning I append Table 28: a list of some further reports that it is

Table 28

Suggested report outputs	
Organisational blockages	Bosses not performing as well as their subordinates and with less recognised potential
By location, department and average age	
By location, department, grade and average salary	Can also be adapted to group by gender or ethnic origin
Current jobs held by employees	Can be adapted to include department and manager
Direct reports to employees	
Job risk A or B	With or without a successor identified
Level A or B performers	With or without a successor identified
Listing of current performance and potential of all employees	
Overdue appraisals or succession review	
Appraisal and potential ratings by location and grade	can group by job risk, succession probability, succession, or none
Employees identified as successors to other jobs	By location and department. Could include succession planned for job outside of department or different location
Summary of performance reviews	By department
Summary and count of ratings given	By appraising manager
Poor performers	With and without successors, by location and department
Potential by performance rating	(Shows up anomalies in performance: potential)
Profile by age, grade, gender and ethnic origin	

possible to get from the database which the user might find useful as a stimulus for developing relevant reports for his or her own organisation. It cannot be a complete list of all possible reports, of course, but is intended to give some ideas for the sort of information that might be useful.

9

DEVELOPMENT-PLANNING

AND CAREER MANAGEMENT

The RDBMS as evolving throughout this book should allow an organisational development manager to spend useful time analysing careers to date and identifying the experience required by individuals to enable them to progress their careers. However, what has not been talked about up to this point are training or development needs not included within the core competencies. This chapter explores ways in which such data can be included and managed by the database in order to produce usable report outputs. Similarly, many organisations employ management trainees and/or modern apprentices – an activity that represents a substantial investment for many companies, and one that needs to be monitored. This chapter illustrates one way in which it can be done, using career-progression graphs.

Organisational development needs

In the appraisal management chapter and the chapter identifying and measuring organisational competencies we looked at ways to assess the abilities of individuals within the identified competencies. Identifying a gap between a competent performance and a competence level that fell short of the competence requirement enabled us to undertake an analysis of the data, to produce a set of reports for the agreed competencies of each employee's job, both graphically for an overall picture, and by way of reports for groups of competency level. By interrogating the database we can identify all of the staff that are in a job, or already chosen as a successor to a job, who have a rating of 1 or 2 for any of the competencies that are listed as the ten key competencies for the job. Remember that a competency of 1 equates to no knowledge, and a competency of 2 equates to an ability only to undertake the job with supervision. This gives us a measure of the training needs for the competency area of the business requirement using the job competencies as the basis. In the chapter on competencies it was suggested that there might be additional competencies that an employee might possess which were not part of the competencies identified for his or her current job. A similar set of reports can be produced for these extra competencies. The organisation may wish to classify them as second order needs because they are not perceived as core competencies for the current job.

This is only part of the story when undertaking an analysis of the training and development needs of the business. There are at least three other major types of information that must be taken into consideration when formulating an organisation plan. These are: the strategic business plan, the departmental business and operating plan, and other needs identified at the appraisal.

The strategic business plan will include longer-term plans for the business which will undoubtedly involve some requirements for the abilities of certain employees of the organisation to change. Although the strategic plan of the organisation will by its very nature be somewhat conceptual and abstract, it will at least give the development manager an awareness of the future plans of the business and the changes that may be necessary.

Perhaps the best way to illustrate the influences of the long-term strategic plan is by example.

At the beginning of the current revolution in desktop computing it became the strategic policy of a major blue-chip food producer to: 'Make maximum use of low-cost computer technology within the organisation, using off-the-shelf software where possible.' As the reader will probably appreciate, this short statement led to a huge investment in both hardware and software: desktop computers proliferated in all parts of the business. This escalation took at least three years, and was slow to start with because few people understood the power of the machine. Initially it was seen as a replacement for the electric typewriter and little else. The training and development manager of the organisation had access to the strategic business plan of the business and was expected to produce an annual report on the ramifications of that plan in relation to development plans for the business. In the case in point, the development manager had to undertake an analysis of what could be done by the computers, what software would be best, and who would be most likely to use the resource. The organisation had decided at the outset that it would limit its software purchasing to three packages, and that they would support these packages only, with technical back-up. The packages were a word-processing package, a spreadsheet package and a database package. All of the chosen packages were brand leaders at the time.

The problem faced by the development manager was to discern the needs of an organisation for development in an area that most of the employees did not yet know that they had any need in.

An analysis of the likely users and the development possibilities of the computers identified

- users who would be using the package as supplied or using applications developed by others
- users who would develop applications for their own use
- users who would develop applications for their own use and the use of other employees
- users who would probably not use the computers but would manage staff who would, or would specify or receive output from the computers.

Who would need training in the respective areas was assessed by job and by level within the organisation. For example: it was obvious that secretaries and clerical workers would need training in word-processing, both at a basic level and at a more advanced level. Department supervisors, project managers, finance supervisors and similar were identified as requiring level 1 training in spreadsheets. Project engineers and logistics supervisors were identified as needing advanced spreadsheet training. The use of database software was rare, so training was not initially undertaken by any staff on the package except for staff in the MIS department and the development manager. The department managers and other senior managers were identified as system definers. They needed to understand what could be done but did not need to know how to do it. At this stage of knowledge of the functions of word-processing people were not generally aware of the things that are now taken for granted, such as spell-checkers and cut-and-paste functions.

Following this analysis of the likely uses of the software and the likely categories of users in the organisation, it was a case of determining which employees would be attending which components of the development programme. Because the whole exercise was about the introduction of computers and the mainframe personnel database at the time was largely confined to payroll administration (using a batch-processing technique that was expensive to reprogram and often not able to make the links possible in a relational database), the selection of employees to attend the various elements of the development programme had to be done manually. With an up-to-date RDBMS such as we have been describing in this book it would be possible to undertake a rapid analysis of likely candidates and to check it with the department managers. To run such a set of queries would be a case of identifying such parameters as

- job class: clerical, technical, administrative, craft, operative
- job level: operative, supervisor, manager, department manager, senior manager, executive.

These two data fields could very well be added to the job details table: they would give two powerful classifications by which to sort jobs or undertake query interrogation.

By undertaking the analysis of the HR information system in this way, a development manager can make the best use of the data available and develop a long-term strategic training plan that can be costed out and built into the training and development budget. Of course it will be necessary to check out how appropriate the plan is when the departmental business plan is discussed in relation to the shorter-term development plan. The foregoing analysis will allow the development manager to make sensible estimates rather than guess at future requirements. The information cannot be derived from the organisational managers because they will not at the time be aware of the need and will not have been able to plan for their own departments. Furthermore, because of the strategic nature of the exercise the information could not be derived through appraisal. Such an analysis may not, in any event, be meaningful for every department.

Amending the composition of existing data tables

It is possible to amend existing data tables by adding and deleting fields. Existing records will then contain blank entries for newly inserted fields – but be careful: data will be lost if existing fields are deleted. It is worth spending a little time to explain how the addition of the two new data fields suggested in the last section could best be undertaken. It is a simple matter of opening the job details data table in a design view or construction mode and simply adding the job class and job level data fields. But for ease of entry we need to consider how to store the data. Because both fields are going to be limited to entries from a definitive list it is best to number each choice and enter an identifying number into the data field. The system can look up the corresponding value for each field when it is producing report output and convert it to a text form that the user can readily understand. Doing this saves storage space and input time. The easiest way to achieve this in a Windows package is to set up two new data tables, one for job class and the other for job level. This has several advantages to the user and the system.

By setting up tables as illustrated overleaf in Tables 29 and 30, we can introduce a range of parameters that will allow even more sophisticated interrogation and also make sure that these are the only values that can be entered into the system. If you are familiar with the Windows™ operating system you will be aware of the ability to click on a drop-down box and select from a list the entry that you wish the system to act on for you. Setting up two drop-down boxes linked to the job class

Table 29
JOB CLASS TABLE

ID NUM	CLASS ID
I	OPERATIVE
2	OPERATIVE SKILLED
3	CRAFT SKILLED
4	CLERICAL
5	ADMINISTRATIVE
6	TECHNICAL
7	PROFESSIONAL
8	PROCESS-BASED

Table 30
JOB LEVEL TABLE

ID NUM	LEVEL ID
I	EMPLOYEE
2	PROCESS CONTROLLER
3	SUPERVISOR
4	IST LINE MANAGER
5	DEPARTMENT MANAGER
6	SENIOR MANAGER
7	EXECUTIVE MANAGER

field and the job level field respectively is the easiest way to enter the data into the existing job details table and also to complete the data for any new jobs entered in the future. This process ensures consistency of data entry, and because the drop-down boxes are linked to a table, new job class and job level definitions can be added at any time. Current definitions should not be amended or deleted because this will create orphan data in the job details table – that is, data that has no relational field to associate with.

The departmental business and operating plan
A further source for the development manager to gather development information from is the departmental business and operating plan. If an organisation is operating properly, the development manager (or person responsible for development) ought to be present at the construction of the plan, or at the very least at the unveiling of the plan. It is this departmental-level process that translates the organisational strategies and business planning process into reality: it is the working out of

what will need to be done and by whom in order to achieve the business goals and objectives. The implementation of the plan may not always involve major change but it will inevitably identify some development needs that will have to be addressed. The issues that will arise from carrying out the plan will include anything from the acquisition of new equipment to the reorganisation of the department, from major project work to individual job realignment. At the earliest possible stage the development of staff will have to be taken into account in order to cope with the changes. It is amazing how many major projects are undertaken, costing millions of pounds, in which no provision is made for training the staff. The presence of specialist HRM staff to assist in identifying the development needs incurred by the changes will help the organisation to concentrate its development budget in priority areas. The debate should be held at an appropriate level in the organisation, at an appropriate time, thus allowing the subsequent prioritised budget to be confirmed. For a large project there ought to be a separate budget for development; it should not usually come within the general development budget.

Development needs identified via the development component of appraisal

The final means by which business development needs are generally identified is the appraisal system. If an employee has a development need that the appraising manager feels is sufficiently important to try to resolve, it is usually entered on the appraisal form. It should be entered as a 'symptom' rather than as a 'cure'. This will allow the development staff to utilise their expertise and investigate the best way to cure the symptom. A symptom may well be expressed as 'uncomfortable when giving direct feedback to subordinates'. All too often this is expressed as 'needs a communication skills course' on the appraisal form. It may well be that such a course would be useful, but there could be better options that will cure the symptom more effectively than that suggestion made on the appraisal form.

Analysing and categorising development needs data

Although this is a book about how the use of computers and information technology can aid the HRM function, it has to be said that computers are not a panacea: at this stage in their development they are not able to do everything. For gathering data to compile a development plan there is no substitute for human intelligence and the human ability to translate the messages received from the input sources, whether from the strategic business plan, from the departmental operational plan or from appraisal forms. At the end of the day the development specialist has got to read the development needs section of the appraisal form in order to analyse the data. The reader will have realised by now that really all the computer brings to the process is an ability to sort data, select data and make calculations on data. For that analysis to have any eventual meaning to us depends on our ability to categorise the development needs data and in some way try to prioritise it.

A good way to try to achieve this is to seek to influence the way in which the data is recorded in the first place. In the example given previously, concerning the introduction of computers into an organisation, such a categorisation took place. It could have been further enhanced by the addition of a data field that identified the priority of the development to the department or individual and/or a date by which the development should be carried out. Such categorisation could be undertaken simultaneously with the other methods of needs identification that have been outlined.

Leaving aside development aligned to a major project, let us consider how we could classify and categorise the development needs of an organisation. Eventually, even a departmental plan has to come down to identifying individual development needs, and it will also be at this stage that data would be entered into the computer. What are the parameters that we need to enter? Certainly they include the proposed action to satisfy the need, the priority of the need, the date by which it should be completed, and perhaps a code defining the method. With this in mind, the design of the development needs section of the appraisal document could be laid out to facilitate the input process. Table 31 represents an illustration of this.

The first two columns of the form would be for information

Table 3 1

	To be completed by appraising manager			To be completed by HRM	
	Development need	priority	Date needed by	Proposed action	action type
1					
2					
3					

only. The four columns to the right would be the basis of the input data to the system: the first two would be filled in by the manager. The date needed by entry is self-explanatory. The priority classification needs an associated definition. A suggestion would be

1   essential to job
2   useful to job
3   longer-term use
4   non-essential.

In exactly the way described previously, a drop-down list could be set up to ensure consistency. The final two columns should be manually completed by the development manager. Both of these could utilise a drop-down list as well. The action type could contain categories for

1   in house course
2   external course
3   external course and accommodation
4   job expansion
5   secondment
6   project work
7   mentoring.

The entries could be made on the form by number, thus minimising time spent by the manager.

The proposed action data field will need to be more carefully thought out, but it is still possible to use the drop-down list input box approach for much of the input. It is probably fair to say that most organisations sponsor a number of development initiatives each year. Some companies even operate a menu system from which development programmes are selected. In that event a data list can be set up that includes in it the major choices available. The current menu of sponsored programmes should reflect the identified needs of the organisation and should therefore cope with most of them. The list will probably include such development areas as specific management or supervisory skills which are not included in the core competencies but which may in fact contribute to the achievement of a competency. Skills training such as in word-processing, specific job-related development for operatives such as operator training for a particular process, NVQ programmes – any identified need that does not fall within the categories previously identified can be added to the list either at the time of entry, if the development manager is undertaking the data entry, or at some other time by a qualified person. Table 32 shows a suggested list-box that could be used as the input mechanism. It could of course be adapted or expanded as required.

Something like this section of the appraisal form could also be produced as a separate form for use when undertaking the strategic analysis or the training needs analysis of the departmental plans. Any additional development types identified in these processes that had not been included in the development events table could be easily added and then entered into the individual's record through the drop-down list facility.

Table 32

1	APPRAISAL INTERVIEWING
2	APPRAISAL PROCESSES
3	SELECTION INTERVIEWING
4	LEADERSHIP SKILLS
5	COACHING SKILLS
6	DECISION-MAKING SKILLS
7	PROBLEM-SOLVING AND ANALYTICAL SKILLS
8	HEALTH AND SAFETY FOR SUPERVISORS
9	FINANCE FOR NON-FINANCIAL MANAGERS
10	SALES FORECASTING SKILLS
11	SALES SKILLS (PRODUCT-SPECIFIC)
12	REPORT WRITING
13	TRAIN THE TRAINER PROGRAM
14	KEY OPERATOR TRAINING (PROCESS-SPECIFIC)

This may at the outset appear to be an arduous task – but much of the work is undertaken in smaller sections by different people. The development manager would in reality only have to fill in the two columns on the hard-copy form. With luck, the data entry would be made by an input operator.

Although there seems a lot of work to be done in managing a development plan, much of the development plan of most organisations will have been carried out in the past, manually. There should really not be a great deal of extra work involved now to reap the benefits of putting the data in a format in which it can be analysed and managed by the RDBMS. The best way to control the input of the data would be to set up another data table for development needs. Table 33 gives an example. Most of the fields in the table are self-explanatory in relation to explanations in previous sections.

Extracting the required information from the database

Having undertaken the analyses that have been outlined including the analysis of job and individual competencies, you now have a wealth of data in the database to produce some valid and useful information reports which will allow the identification of development needs for individuals, for departments and by subject area. It will be possible to produce reports which identify suitable methods for the development of the required skills and the order of priority in which these should be undertaken for the benefit of the business. Extracting this level of complexity of information features exactly the same process as has been used earlier: querying the database. The difference now is only the number of tables it is necessary to link in order to get the information. Suppose

Table 33

EMPLOYEE NUMBER
ENTRY DATE
IDENTIFIED NEED NUMBER
PRIORITY LEVEL   (NUMERIC CODE FROM A DEFAULT ENTRY LIST)
PROPOSED METHOD   (NUMERIC CODE FROM DEFAULT ENTRY LIST)
DATE TO BE DONE BY

we need to pick out all those employees who have been identified as capable of development in the leadership of people, a query can be built up linking a number of tables that would provide us with prioritised information upon which to base the development plan.

Figure 12 shows the tables it would be necessary to link in order to ask the database the question. The best way to understand the query is to go through the tables and work out what data will be extracted, and how, and then to look at the parameters that we might wish to set.

The first table from which we need to extract data is the employee details table. We get the employee's name from this: only the surname has been extracted here, but the forename could easily be extracted also. Most importantly, we have extracted the employee number – the link through to many of the other tables, although we may choose not to exhibit the number. The job details table gives us the job title, department, location, job class and job level, as well as the job number. The job number allows us to link the query to the job core competencies table and to the key competencies name table. The link to the key competencies name table enables us to substitute the competency number in the core competencies

Figure 12

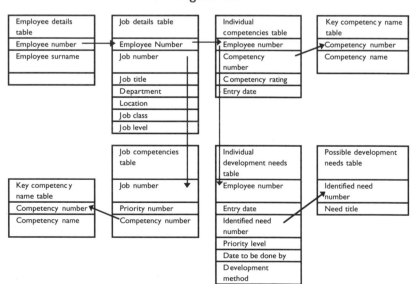

table for the actual name of the competency. The link from the job details employee number to the individual competency table is via the employee number, thus enabling the query to reach in and find the individual competency level of staff within jobs. The name of the competency is arrived at by the same method as in the previous example. The employee number then links to the individual development needs table in order to get information about the training needs identified via the appraisal, the strategic plan or the departmental plan. The data is held by number, but the link to the possible development needs table enables the name of the need to be identified.

If this query were to be run in this form it would generate information about every need, every job and every competency. What we need to do is to qualify the information that we require.

The information can be qualified by identifying the parameters of the query and entering them in the appropriate way for the RDBMS that is being used. If the user requires all of the details about one person, it would be necessary to enter the employee number of that person in the criteria statement section of the employee number in the employee details table. This would show the competencies required for the job, the employee's ability in all of the competency areas identified, and any other needs identified as relevant to this person. By adding a further calculated data field column to the query, it would be possible to show the performance variance between the required job competencies and the individual's rated job competencies.

Of more use to the organisation would be the ability to query by development need. This could be achieved by the same basic query, but it would be necessary to change the selection criteria from the last example. Suppose on this occasion we want to pick out all the staff within the organisation who have some need for development in their leadership skills. The easiest way to achieve this would be to enter into the criterion box of the job competency table, the individual competence table and the individual development needs table the identifying number of any job competence or development need that is associated to the skill of leadership. For example: competency 4 in the competency table and development need 4 in the drop-down list for individual development needs would give details of all staff who have a need in this area.

By producing a standardised report, the data can be grouped by location, department, job level, job class and individual. The report can also show the priority level of the development.

Such analysis gives a powerful tool to the development department with which to ensure that the development that is most relevant to the needs of the business is that which is concentrated upon.

This type of query is very powerful – but it would be most inconvenient if the process I have described had to be undertaken every time that a user wished to compile a query relating to a particular need. Instead, the user should set up a basic query like the one described above, but rather than put in the actual query criterion (leadership in the example), should make use of the facility by which the system allows a blank criterion statement to be entered into any data field in the query which the user can complete at the time of making the query. Whenever the query is run, the system will prompt for the competency and the development need to be entered. A report on any need can thus be produced just by entering the criteria. This facility is one of the greatest attractions of a RDBMS – a query and report have to be set up only once and then the reports on any criteria can be run at any time.

Refinements to the above query are limited only by the imagination of the user. A further refinement that would be most useful when calculating the annual development budget is to get the system to report the development needs not by individual name but by counting the number of staff with the need and just reporting the total for each grouping. The above report could therefore still be produced by department, location, level, class and identified need, but it would just indicate the number of people in each group and an overall total. This could be a godsend for budgeting.

The reader should perhaps take some time at this point to digest this section. It constitutes the greatest reason for storing data, being able to manipulate it and turning it into selective information. The concept is somewhat difficult to take in – it is far more mechanical than the way in which human beings tend to think. Try thinking about how you would use this approach in your own organisation. Remember: it does not have to be as comprehensive as this to start with. Provided that the links have been made or the ability to make them has been built in, new tables can be added at any time.

Career-planning

All too often it is assumed that there is a training solution to every problem. It is simply not the case. Likewise, it is even less the case that there is a training course solution to every problem. One of the misunderstandings in the past about appraisal has been that once a problem has been identified and written on the appraisal form it becomes someone else's problem to solve – notably the HRM department's. A shift in development techniques has taken place over the last few years as organisations have undergone dramatic reorganisation. Cash for training has been tighter than ever. Different techniques have been accepted by managers to develop staff. The last section concerned the identification of development needs, but there was no intended implication in it that every need should have a training solution. Certainly, many identified needs will have a training component attached to their resolution, probably more at the knowledge-gaining level. Valuable development techniques such as secondment, mentoring, project group work and focus groups can be utilised to develop skill and ability beyond the knowledge-acquisition stage. These techniques have been used by staff development managers for a long time, and there is nothing revolutionary in suggesting their use in this book. What the book can introduce, however, is the accessibility of the means to identify situations, people or jobs that may enable an individual to develop his or her career potential. Look at the data that we have gathered about the employees within our organisation. We know what everybody does and we know how well they do it. We know how well people are expected to perform and develop. We also know what individual strengths and weaknesses there are in terms of job competencies, as well as individual training needs. We know the level at which they operate within the organisation, where they are based and what departments they are in. We know all of this and more, for good performers and bad performers. As we shall discuss in the next chapter, we can also access a record of all training and development that has been undertaken by individuals. Linking some of this data together, we can make a valuable contribution to the business – perhaps by identifying people in the organisation with particular strengths that they may be able to pass on to other people as mentors or as members of development project groups and focus groups. The database will give details of any actual training undertaken by individuals, whether on or off the job. It has always been difficult to transfer the learning from formal training back to the workplace. One way is to set up career-management groups who can discuss the event and assist each other to take advantage of the training. The RDBMS itself will not make such events happen, but it can help HRM manage the processes. Hopefully, by now the reader will see the benefits of formally storing data in a computer rather than on separate sheets in a hard-copy form. Such paper-based systems are not dynamic – it is not possible to make the links across the system that can be made with a computerised system as described here.

Career-development graphs

As a final section to this chapter let us look at how a career-development plan can be constructed for an individual and how its progress can be monitored both independently and against requirement.

Our approach is to trace the path of a graduate management trainee or an employee undertaking a modular-based experiential NVQ. And our explanation of it is based on the appointment of a graduate trainee. Many organisations accept an annual intake of graduate management trainees. Although in the early 1990s that trend diminished, it is now in the latter part of the decade starting to flourish again. Of course it is an essential part of an organisation's investment in the future to take on and train staff, including the people who are expected one day to become senior managers. What it is difficult to accept, given current data-processing technology, is the practice of taking on such an employee without some analysis of future need or, indeed, a long-term potential target position for the person. This is not to say that a particular individual could be taken on specifically to be marketing director within ten years, but it ought to be possible to anticipate that this person should be capable of that or a similar job within the organisation in an identified timespan.

Trainees of any variety are not a small investment for an organisation. It is therefore crucial that people taken on under a graduate scheme should have career targets to aim at and to achieve throughout their careers. The organisation must also have a payback for its investment. Developing an individual to be able to deliver that payback is important. It is also important to be able to assess whether or not the person is going to achieve a target by the time predicted, or indeed whether he or she is ahead of schedule.

Such long-term planning and monitoring is something that can be done using the techniques and tools of HRM discussed within this book. I am not suggesting that trainees should be cosseted or spoon-fed: they must earn their corn like everyone else. However, it is unlikely that they add value to the organisation for the first one or two years. They may join the company with good qualifications but they are unlikely to have much experience. It is that experience and company knowledge that must be developed in the first two years. After this period of time it is normal for graduates to have to fend for themselves within the organisation. It is the role of the development department to manage the career of the graduate trainee in just the same way as it is his or her role to manage everyone else's potential. If the recruitment of the trainee was correct in the first place, the trainee's abilities should continue to merit a 'B' or 'A' rating for performance and potential.

Career-tracking is a way of describing to employees the sorts of experiences and accountabilities they should have as they progress through their careers. It is defined in six-monthly objectives, and should consist of an achievement statement that describes a satisfactory performance during that period. In the example overleaf (Table 34) we track a graduate trainee's expected development path through to a senior HRM role in a multidivisional company over a five-year period. The targets are identified in six-month periods.

Each of the sections within this five-year plan show a progression in terms of increasing accountability. These can in fact be viewed as the individual competencies required for this job. They are all stated in terms of output, and the skills required to do them are therefore implicit in the job: the normal requirements of the organisation's identified core competencies are implicitly included. At the end of each six-month period, the individual trainee can be rated against the same set of ratings that were used for assessing core competencies in Chapter 7:

1   No ability in this competency
2   Able to undertake this competency under supervision
3   Able to undertake this competency without supervision
4   Able to assist or supervise peer-group members to undertake this competency.

The trainee would be expected to achieve at least a level 3 rating at the end of each six-month period. The experiences

Table 34

Months in company	GRADUATE MANAGEMENT TRAINEE HRM DEPT Expected achievement for the period
6	Understand and operate the HRM procedures of the company. Analyse vacancy requirement and undertake operative recruitment at a production site.
12	Analyse the constituent parts of national pay negotiation and develop a computerised model that identifies the true cost to the organisation of any pay award. Manage the processes of the negotiations (venue, agenda, minutes, etc)
18	Manage a sector of the HRM department to agreed performance target levels.
24	Learn and manage a sector of the business other than HRM. Produce budget forecast.
30	Manage a local HRM department at a company production location remote from head office.
36	As previous six months.
42	Be able to carry out supervisory skills training to an agreed level.
48	Be accountable for producing the organisational employee development plan, and develop and agree training budget.
52	Develop departmental strategic plan. Develop and agree overall departmental budget.
60	Control an HRM discipline in the head office environment: eg pay and rewards, HRD, resourcing.

shown in the table are representative of the level of experience required by the individual to stay on track. After the initial training period it will not be possible to state categorically what the individual will or will not be doing so far in advance. Who knows what the business needs might be?

Assuming that a trainee achieves a level 3 rating all the way through the five-year period of career monitoring, it would be possible to plot a straight-line graph showing it. Figure 13 shows how actual progress might look for two trainees plotted on a graph against the expected straight-line progression. We can see that candidate 1 after eighteen months starts to dip below the straight line to the extent that it is doubtful if he or she will ever make the target appointment level. This gives the HRM department and the department manager of the trainees' discipline (in the example it is HRM) an early indicator at a glance of the potential of an individual. They can then make decisions regarding the employee's future with the company. This type of supporting material is increasingly being asked for in tribunal cases, although it can only be supporting information in such an event: it does not obviate the need to undertake the required disciplinary procedures if a decision is made not to pursue the employment. Equally, the organisation may take the view that the employee could still make a valuable contribution to the business, but not at the previously anticipated level. Candidate 2 poses the opposite problem: he or she

Figure 13

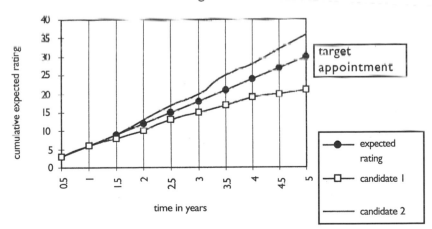

is over-achieving. This may create just as much of a problem as the underachiever; only individual business managers can make this decision. Of course the business might be very happy to have a fast-track employee who will be ready to take on a job at the target level before the anticipated time.

The graph can be produced from within most RDBMS packages. If that is not possible, however, it certainly will be possible to export the data and produce the graph in a spreadsheet package. The time taken to produce the graphs is negligible, provided that the data is entered into a table every six months. The system can calculate the cumulative ratings and plot them onto a graph for each trainee. This method has as much value in relation to trainees undertaking modern apprenticeships as it does to the example given, especially if an organisation needs to keep track of a fair number of trainees.

That concludes this chapter on using the computer to aid career-planning. Some of the concepts are not easy to grasp, and of course they will not suit all organisations. The purpose of the chapter is as much to stimulate thought as it is to define an approach.

10

MANAGING TRAINING

AND DEVELOPMENT

We have already looked at ways in which we can identify the training and development needs of employees within the organisation. Now we look at ways in which that information can be used by the development department, and at ways in which the development department can use information technology to enhance its performance within the organisation, ways of managing events, and ways of analysing events and whole programmes. We look at useful variables that can be stored in the database to help the department to measure itself and its contribution to the business, and we examine how to keep training records and link them to the identified needs.

So far we have entered a great deal of data into our Human Resource Information System. It may even seem that there is a danger of overkill. Yet the amount of data entered so far is no more than an effective business needs to store about its staff. Certainly, if all of the data had to be entered by one person, and all at once, it would be a daunting task. However, this will never be the case – and besides, data entry into the system can be carried out in several ways. First it is most likely that the system will be accessed by a number of authorised users. Even on a single machine, data is usually entered into the system by several people according to their own sphere of interest in the process. In a small number of cases, however, data entry may fall to one person. Yet even then, not all of the data will be entered at one time. Some data may be entered via a scanner, as outlined previously. The point is that there are many rewards for the HRM department in taking the time to enter the data, and so recording the HR history of the company. The value of the data to the process of managing training and development should become clear during this chapter.

Managing development events

Chapter 9 looked at ways of identifying training and development needs and how to store data about those needs in the system in a way that would allow the system to be interrogated. There is no need to go back over this stage of the formulation of a development plan. We have already looked at the methodology that can be employed to prioritise development needs of individuals and departments. Using this data, we can produce a training and development plan for the whole organisation, by topic and in priority order, for each individual within each need category. What this does not do is identify the overall priorities of the business in deciding which training and development events are to be held during the coming budgeting period. In an ideal world we would seek to resolve all the identified needs, but the economic realities of running a business mean that the individual development needs that match priority needs of the business have the greatest chance of being resolved. Individual needs that are rated as high priority by the individual but less so by the business have less chance of being attended to. This is not a criticism but rather a recognition of reality. In some organisations the development department may be criticised as not being in touch with the needs of the business in respect of the staff development that is put in hand. After implementing a system of analysis as described in this book, and which involves the organisational managers to the fullest extent, a development manager can answer any such criticism by producing information that has been collated from data supplied by the business itself. Having produced such development needs data in collated form, the development manager must then agree with the senior managers of the organisation which of the identified programmes is of most benefit to the organisation. This level of organisational involvement ensures that the development that is undertaken will, as far as possible, coincide with the needs of the organisation. Remember, though, that not all development has a training solution, and much of the individual development can be undertaken by low-cost internal methods such as mentoring and secondment. A further limitation on the department will always be the size of the training budget. It is not possible to generalise about the amount of money an organisation spends on its training and development. Most development managers would probably argue that they need more: reality dictates that more is rarely forthcoming. At least by prioritising in the ways suggested, an organisation should be able to say that – irrespective of the size of the budget – the best use has been made of it. Chapter 11 looks at how a budget can be built up using a computer; the example used is the formulation of a development budget.

Let us suppose, then, that the organisation has identified the development events it wishes to sponsor for the coming budget period. How can the computer help to manage these

Table 35
ADDITIONAL DATA TABLES FOR MANAGING DEVELOPMENT EVENTS

EVENT DETAILS TABLE
EVENT CODE NUMBER
EVENT DATE
EVENT TITLE
VENUE CODE
START TIME
DURATION
RESIDENTIAL
FINISH TIME
FINISH DATE
CONSULTANT ID NUM
INTERNAL TRAINER EMP NUM

ATTENDEES TABLE
EVENT CODE NUMBER
DELEGATE'S EMPLOYEE NUMBER
ATTENDANCE CONFIRMATION

VENUE TABLE
VENUE CODE
EVENT VENUE NAME
EVENT ADDRESS 1
EVENT ADDRESS 2
EVENT TOWN
EVENT POSTCODE
EVENT PHONE NUM
EVENT FAX NUM
24-HR RATE
CONFERENCE RATE
ENTRY DATE

CONSULTANT DETAILS TABLE
CONSULTANT ID NUM
CONSULTANT NAME
HOME ADDRESS
HOME PHONE
DAY RATE
ENTRY DATE

events? To assist us to manage the process it will be necessary to set up the four data tables shown in Table 35. These are not very large tables, but they will be important in what they allow us to manage.

The main table is the event details table. This could be used for every development activity that is undertaken – even one-to-one sessions or secondment – but this would probably create a mammoth task and might well incur criticism from the business about overinvolvement in informal events. The table is set up to record formal development events which require off-the-job methods. The rationale behind the data field names should by this time be easy for the reader to understand. The event code number links to the attendees table, and thus allows us to identify delegates by name, using a further link to the details table. The delegates attending can be drawn from the reports identifying individual development needs. It is probably quicker to key in the delegate employee number than to develop an automatic system. A drop-down list-box could easily enter the details although it would take some time to go through all the employees in the list. By using manual keying-in it is easier to make any changes that need to be made as result of date conflicts. It is likely that most organisations will use a number of venues to undertake training activities. By entering these in a small table it saves the details from being entered into each event. If training is actually given on site, that too can be entered as a venue code together with the other details. The reason will be explained in a short while.

There are two fields that can be used to identify the person to conduct the development event: one for an external trainer, and one for an internal trainer. The irrelevent field can be left blank..

The consultant details table holds the details of external consultants who might be used by the organisation. It links to the consultant identity number field in the event details table, thus enabling us to log the use of any consultants brought in by the company. The entry date field enables us to distinguish fee changes through time. We could also do this by setting up another linked table, but this will serve just as well. For similar reasons the venue table has the date field in it.

With this small amount of data we can now start to produce a number of reports. Possibly the most important of them will be the course-joining instructions for the delegates and the instructions to the trainer or consultant. The data held in the system allows us to send joining instructions to inform each delegate of the event title, time, place, venue, duration, proposed finish time, trainer details, and whether the course is residential or not. Because we need to enter the venue in the joining instructions, we must identify the on-site course location as a venue in the venue table. The system will also be able to extract from other tables the delegates' internal or external addresses. It will be able to send a copy of the joining instructions to each employee's immediate manager; it could even give details of the agenda of a pre-course meeting to be held between the manager and the delegate. This should help to prevent the delegates arriving for the programme from saying that they know nothing about it or that their manager has not mentioned it to them. The same data will be able to generate a list of course details and delegate details to the consultant, including the delegates' name, job titles and organisational locations. Similarly a list of delegates and trainers could be supplied to the hotel.

All of these reports could be generated by a macro (a small program embedded in the system) that has been prepared in advance and that will produce the details for any program at any time. The advantage to the development department is that the macro has to be written only once, the report output layouts only have to be prepared once, and simply by running a macro – often by using a defined single-keystroke short-cut – the entire set of course-joining instructions as described can be produced. For the most part the only input requirement is the completion of the event details table and the attendees table for each event.

Assuming that the attendees table and the event details table are completed following the authorisation of the annual training budget, it would be easy to produce a planned development event report which could be produced by department and/or location for the forthcoming year. This could then be circulated to every department, thus affording an opportunity to make any changes required to the proposed programme.

After the event

So far we have seen how the attendance of events can be managed – which in itself represents a big step forward, compared with some of the systems I have seen in operation. A system like this should at least prevent an employee attending the same programme twice – as has been known to happen in the past. The system can be made to prompt the user if an employee gets entered to attend the same type of event twice by linking the event code number to the individual training need: it would then show that the identified event had already occurred in relation to an identified need of the delegate.

At the end of most development events delegates are asked to complete a questionnaire about the programme. There are varying views about the usefulness of the data that is gained from this process, yet such questionnaires tend to be the norm. What happens to the data? In most cases, very little. But if the questionnaire was constructed in a way that made entry into a database easy, it could be a useful source of appropriate data. By using forced-choice questions or rating scales from 1 to 10, a picture of the quality of venue, interpersonal skills of trainers, satisfaction with the course administration, quality of the prebriefing processes, etc, could be built up. Over time an analysis of this data could give the organisation useful feedback about the areas on the questionnaire. The return of the questionnaire could also be the source by which the input data field confirms attendance of the event in the attendees table. It would be necessary to set up a data table to deal with the data from the questionnaires. It would vary depending on the questions asked, but it could be constructed to ensure that the values entered fell within the acceptable input parameters of the form. It could also be scanned into the system to save employee's time.

Similarly, a post-course questionnaire could be devised that could be sent to the delegate – perhaps after six weeks had elapsed. The system could generate the questionnaire or a report prompting the department to send a questionnaire. Here again it would be necessary to devise a standard forced-choice or scalar-value-range set of questions that gave statistical information about the validity of the event, the quality of the event and the effectiveness of the event. Just as the first questionnaire was, this second questionnaire could be entered into a data table. Both of these tables could have data fields that allow links to be made either to the individual or the event. Analysis through time of the questionnaires should enable a qualitative assessment to be made of the various aspects of the development events that have been surveyed. It should enable an organisation to assess whether it is getting a satisfactory standard of service from development providers. The questionnaire could also prompt each delegate and his or her manager to have a post-event meeting and to devise an action plan to implement the development event content. This could also be confirmed as having happened on the questionnaire. The return of the questionnaire would be a requirement: the system would prompt – or even produce a reminder – if the data from the questionnaire was not entered into the system within ten weeks of the end of the event. This is not meant to sound like a policing operation. The system does 'enforce' the process, but it is necessary to ensure that the organisation gets the best value for money it can from its development budget.

Appraisal time

In the chapter on appraisal it was suggested that the system should produce an individual appraisal form for each employee. The usefulness of this becomes even more apparent with the inclusion of previous data regarding identified development needs, identified competency levels and development undertaken during the period being appraised. Although an employee might have attended a development programme during the year, it cannot be assumed that the development need has been satisfied. This can only be ascertained by asking the manager appraising the individual to confirm the level of competence now held by the employee. When a development need has been satisfied, a box can be ticked on the system-generated appraisal form which will then prompt a final entry into the data table indicating that the need has been satisfied. It will also show in the current competency rating, assuming that the need was aligned to a job competency and that the new rating is 3 or 4. The entry of this data would round off the whole development needs analysis of the previous period and allow the analysis of all the development activities undertaken throughout the period. This would include secondments and project events, etc.

With the data now held in the system we can therefore analyse the effectiveness of a single event, a series of events, or the whole development programme. We can compare the relative results of individual course presenters and establish a value-for-money report, particularly beneficial when using external consultants. We can produce actual evidence of the effect that development is having on the organisation by undertaking an annual competence rating comparison analysis on staff who attended formal development. Indeed, we can establish realistic targets for developers to achieve. We can establish the proportion of the budget spent on external consultants and on external development venues. By totalling the number of training days per event and the overall cost of consultant and venue, we can establish a cost per training day per event or overall.

These are measures that would have been difficult to produce without the aid of computers, largely because of the complexity of manual data analysis. With computerised data links it becomes easier for the development department to establish its contribution to the business and for it to argue for a greater emphasis to be placed on development in an organisation. Such information can genuinely help to answer the legitimate questions posed by finance departments when seeking to justify costs.

Many of the examples quoted in this text centre upon the less tangible skills of the organisation – but the principles of the model are equally good when monitoring the tangible skills of a business. By measuring pre-training abilities or product failure rates and then measuring the post-training performance, it is easy to derive an aggregate performance improvement of a number of employees who have undergone a programme of training. The parameters will be peculiar to each example: they will include such factors as shorter time taken to achieve a task, lower failure rate, lower process downtime, lower materials wastage, and lower staff turnover. Criteria like these are probably not in the interests of the organisation to be set up as part of the overall RDBMS, as so far described. It is possible (and more practical) to undertake an analysis using the database capabilities of a spreadsheet. Although such a database is not a relational database, the analytical capabilities of data entered into a two-dimensional spreadsheet are extremely powerful. Microsoft Excel 5 onwards, has a facility called a pivot table that allows the user to undertake a rapid analysis by means of a database which makes comparisons against different data fields, utilising the 'wizard' facility in Excel. Wizards are routines built into Microsoft products that are in effect comprehensive macros, which allow the user to perform complex tasks with a minimum of input. In the example shown below, a two-dimensional spreadsheet database has been set up in Excel 5 which includes the basic details of an organisation's staff, surnames, initials, dates of birth, start dates, grades, salaries and lengths of service. These are easily extracted from the main RDBMS and imported into Excel just for this analysis. One of the advantages of doing an analysis in this way is that the original data is safely stored in another program and cannot get corrupted by any errors made in this analysis. It is also easier to get summarised data without having to set up report formats. The downside is that each time a user wishes to carry out an

Table 36
EXAMPLE OF AN EXCEL PIVOT TABLE

LOCATION	(All)	
Average of SALARY		
DEPARTMENT	Total	
ADMIN		17428
DESPATCH		10142
EXEC		38000
MAINTENANCE		16000
PRODUCTION		11600
R&D		21000
SALES		18857
Average salary		14868

analysis it is necessary to start from scratch. The method is best used for one-off analyses, leaving the more powerful RDBMS reporting facilities for the regular reports.

Table 36 is an example of a pivot table created by Excel. The worksheet from which this pivot table was created contained 99 records. By following the pivot table wizard Excel has produced a summary of the data within the data table that shows for all locations the average salary for each department. To set this up takes less than a minute. Excel then saves the pivot table onto a new worksheet in the open workbook in order that it can be kept as a permanent record.

The calculations that can be done on any numerical data field include totals, averages, variances, the maximum value in a class, the minimum value in a class, the standard deviation and a total count of entries. The pivot table is worth exploring. It does not make sense for all data ranges and types, but where it does it can save the user a lot of time when analysing data on an *ad hoc* basis.

A criticism that has often been levied at the HRM department, and particularly development initiatives, is that there is often no visible payback to the organisation following an investment in development. A computer can be utilised to assist the department to manage the process, thus enhancing the efficiency of that process. Moreover, by using the calculating strength of the computer and its ability to store, manipulate and analyse data, it is possible to build up some useful information that can show the organisation the benefits of undertaking development initiatives.

11

BUILDING AND CONTROLLING

FORECASTS AND BUDGETS

The thought of building a forecast and budget model without the aid of a computer is frightening. Of course there are many ways that such a task can be undertaken even using a computer. This chapter outlines techniques that can be adopted in order to make the process as easy as possible and to utilise much of the data already stored in a HRIS.

The description of the actual budget forecast is based on the spreadsheet format, using Microsoft Excel 5 as an example. The chapter does not set out to teach the use of a spreadsheet: it assumes a basic knowledge of spreadsheets, although explanations of some spreadsheet concepts are given where deemed appropriate.

It is a fact of managerial life that forecasts and budgets, once submitted, usually get returned for revision. In the case of a sales forecast the revision is usually upwards, whereas for a cost budget it is the reverse. Building the models on a spreadsheet can make the amendment process much easier, provided that the model has been thought out in advance. The basic principle of a spreadsheet is to create it so that it can be modified with as few cell value changes as possible. As an example this chapter presents the development of a training and development cost budget which builds a zero-based model from the information held in an RDBMS. Zero-based budgeting is defined as building a budget from scratch, based on all current identified needs. It does not look at what was spent last year as a guide; nor does it take a fixed amount and then identify sufficient training to spend the money. It does not even mean that all the required money will necessarily be forthcoming, either. Rather it is a technique to ensure that the process is looked at with fresh eyes each time and to establish all of the needs before prioritising.

Building up the cost of a training event

One of the greatest assets of a spreadsheet is its ability to copy cells down or across the worksheet. Because we are trying to introduce a standardised approach to the budgeting process we need to identify the components of a development event that influence the ultimate cost of the event. Using the copying power of the spreadsheet means that if we think through the component costs for one type of event we must be able to re-use the criteria for all other sorts of events.

The example that we use below to illustrate the costs involved in running a development programme is based on the data extracted from the database in respect of employees who exhibit a need for basic appraisal skills development. After an interrogation of the database it has been discovered that there are 30 employees with this need. Table 37 shows a screen presentation for this data, together with some other details that I should explain at this point.

The first explanation concerns the code for the course type: 'RH'. This signifies that the course will be run as a residential course in a hotel using an external consultant. There are

Table 37

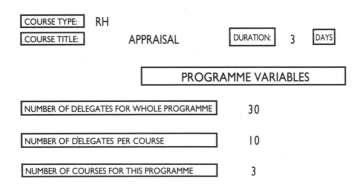

several other codes that it is necessary to set up in order to cover all types of event. These will be explained later. By inputting this code, the spreadsheet has been set up to implement a particular formula for costing out the programme. The course title is self-explanatory, and the user is required to key in the duration of an event in days. The total number of 30 delegates for the programme is entered. The number of delegates per event is set at ten. The computer then calculates that three events are required to satisfy the complete programme. In actual fact, the calculation that the spreadsheet makes to arrive at this is:

(Roundup (Total number of delegates divided by delegates per course)).

The reason for this is that if the limit is ten and there is an odd five, then an additional event will have to be run for that group of five. This will involve the costs of a full course. For the purpose of the example let us keep with easy numbers.

Now consider what is involved in the cost of running a development event in a hotel using an external consultant. With the exception of the textbook costs and external course average costs, Table 38 shows the predicted types of costs that may be involved. In fact, some combination of the factors in

Table 38

EVENT VARIABLES	COST
HOTEL 24-HOUR RATE	120
CONFERENCE DAY RATE	40
CONSULTANT DAY RATE	650
AVERAGE RETURN TRAVEL	50
VIDEO FILM HIRE	200
EQUIPMENT HIRE/COURSE	200
HANDOUTS etc. PER DELEGATE	20
TEXTBOOKS FOR COLLEGE	125
EXTERNAL COURSE AVERAGE COST	1500

this list should cope with forecasting the cost of any formal development event for budgeting purposes.

The table also shows the approximate cost of each factor. Remember that at this stage we are undertaking a forecast for the forthcoming budget year, and although we may not know the exact figure for each item, we need to set aside money to pay for the events when they happen. It may seem strange, therefore, that an amount of £50 is entered for travel expenses per person when some people might travel from London to Edinburgh to attend a course and others may only travel five miles. The best way to achieve a realistic forecast figure for such values as travel is to establish the average travel cost from the previous year or half-year, and enter that amount for every person: what is gained on the swings will be lost on the roundabouts. In common with all of the amounts that feature in Table 38, the travel expense figure is a guide for budgeting and forecasting. It is important to use realistic amounts and to be a little generous. In my experience, actual events never cost less than expected. Although the purpose of the exercise is to forecast an amount of money necessary for a specific purpose, the finance department will be unlikely to allow spending over forecast because the predictions were underestimated.

The first three factors need to be costed per day per person; the remainder are costed per event per person. In order to arrive at the cost of each event, it is a question of arriving at a cost per delegate per programme, multiplying this by the number of delegates, and then adding the cost per course of the external consultant.

To cost out the accommodation per individual delegate for the programme it is necessary first to establish the duration of the programme. The actual duration of the programme is three days, but this only includes two overnight stays. An effective way of helping to control budget spending on a programme is not to have delegates stay overnight on the night before the event. That is not always practical, but for the purposes of developing this model this approach will be used. So the cost of the accommodation per person is two times the 24-hour rate and once at the conference day rate. The 24-hour rate includes all meals and accommodation and usually a

Table 39
COURSE ACCOMMODATION COSTS

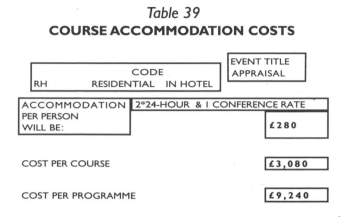

		EVENT TITLE
	CODE	APPRAISAL
RH	RESIDENTIAL IN HOTEL	

ACCOMMODATION PER PERSON WILL BE:	2*24-HOUR & I CONFERENCE RATE	
		£280

COST PER COURSE	£3,080

COST PER PROGRAMME	£9,240

conference room. The conference day rate includes the conference room, lunch, coffee and tea. By adopting this approach we can save £80 per delegate per programme – or the difference between the 24-hour rate and the conference day rate, however much that is. Table 39 shows a representation of a computer screen that has worked out the cost of the accommodation for the appraisal programme.

The screen shows a figure of £280 per delegate for 2*24 hours' accommodation. The cost per course is not ten times the delegate cost but eleven times, since it is normal to include the cost of accommodation for the consultant. Finally, the screen shows the cost of accommodation for the whole programme of appraisal events: £9,240. The figure that we are interested in at the moment is the cost of accommodation for one event of ten people plus the consultant. To

Table 40

APPRAISAL	RESIDENTIAL IN HOTEL	
	COURSE	PROGRAMME
CONSULTANT FEES	£1,950	£5,850
TRAVEL COSTS	£ 550	£1,650
VIDEO HIRE	£ 200	£ 600
EQUIPMENT HIRE	£ 200	£ 600
HANDOUTS etc.	£ 200	£ 600
TEXTBOOKS	£ -	£ 0
COURSE COST	£ -	£ 0
ACCOMMODATION B/FWD	£3,080	£9,240
TOTAL FOR NEED	£6,180	£18,540

establish the total cost for the event we need to add in the cost of the other variables. Table 40 illustrates what these will be in relation to this example.

The screen shows the costs in two columns: the first column is per event, and the second is per programme. We can see that the spreadsheet model is multiplying the daily cost of the consultant by the duration of the programme, the travel costs by the number of delegates plus the consultant, the handouts by the number of delegates. The cost of equipment hire and video hire is entered as the figure in Table 38. Totalling this column and adding that total to the accommodation cost per event shows that the cost per event for running a three-day appraisal programme for ten delegates and using a consultant is £6,180, and the total cost for three events is £18,540. To adjust any of the item costings would only require amending the values in Table 38, since that is the master table.

Every calculation links back to those values by entering the cell address of the appropriate value in each formula in the workbook. If the worksheet formulae use the conventional technique of referring to other cells by their address, it can get complicated and difficult to track – especially when using more than one worksheet in a workbook. By far the easiest way to overcome this problem is to name the cell that holds the values that you will want to refer to. This means that a formula can be referred to by the cell name rather than the address. It is much easier to spot errors if a formula is written as (dayrate * duration) rather than as (Sheet1!$F$10 * Sheet2!$G$8). The reader should read the instruction for the particular spreadsheet package that is being used for details of how to name cells.

Costing the whole budget

Estimating the cost of the whole budget is really an iterative process of estimating the cost of one programme – except that not all programmes will be three-day events for ten people at a time. There will be different types of events involving various combinations of the cost contributors outlined in Table 38.

Table 41 shows a list of different types of events that might be applicable to an organisation which uses various ways to satisfy its formal development needs. Each of these will need a different combination of cost contributors. For example: an event run in-house but using a consultant would not incur accommodation costs, but it would probably incur all the other costs that the appraisal example did (travel may or may not be included). In the example used in this model travel has been included on the assumption that, although the programme is run in-house, the company training centre is at a separate location from the manufacturing sites. This can

Table 41

PROGRAMME TYPE	CODE
RESIDENTIAL & COURSE IN HOTEL	RH
EXTERNAL & ACCOMMODATION	EA
EXTERNAL & NO ACCOMMODATION	EX
IN HOUSE BY CONSULTANT	IC
IN-HOUSE BY OWN STAFF	IO
IN-HOUSE, ACCOM & CONSULTANT	IA
IN-HOUSE, OWN STAFF & ACCOM	IN
COLLEGE COURSE	CO

easily be varied: each of the types of event has a code attached to it. It is this code that is referred to by the application and which then determines the cost contributors that need to be included in the budgeting process.

So far the screen representations that have been shown probably do not look much like a conventional spreadsheet screen to the reader. Nevertheless, that is what they are. They have been developed as input screens for the process of identifying the parameters required to be built in to the model and as illustrators of how to budget a single event, but it would not be much use to us if we had to produce a separate screen for each series of planned events. Table 42 probably looks more

Table 42
BUDGET TOTALS

	CODING	ACCOM	CONSLTNTS	TRAVEL	VIDEO	EQUIP	HANDOUTS	TEXTS	EXTVENES	EVENT TTL	PROG TOTAL
APPRAISAL	RH	3080	1950	550	200	200	200	0	0	6180	18540
ASSERTION	EA	240	0	50	0	0	0	0	1500	1790	5370
FIRST AID	EX	0	0	50	0	0	0	0	1500	1550	4650
WORD PRO	IC	0	1950	550	200	200	200	0	0	3100	9300
SPREADSHEET	IO	0	0	300	200	200	120	0	0	820	2460
RECRUITMENT	IA	2640	1950	550	200	200	200	0	0	5740	17220
SALES SKILLS	IN	1440	0	300	200	200	120	0	0	2260	6780
IPD PROG	CO	0	0	0	0	0	0	125	1500	1625	4875
										23065	69195
COST CENTRE TOTALS		22200	17550	7050	3000	3000	2520	375	13500		

like the type of output screen arrangement that the reader is used to seeing from a spreadsheet package. In reality the top row of the display is giving the same information about the appraisal programme as in the previous example, except that it is laid out differently. The formulae used to achieve it are exactly the same.

Table 42 shows how a complete budget can be built up in the same way that the appraisal example has been. The key to the values used is the coding. For example: the second row shows the cost for one person to attend an assertion skills course run by an external organisation but which includes accommodation. The duration is three days, which implies two nights' accommodation, plus travel and course cost. All of these figures correspond with the standard costing figures entered into Table 38. The event total sums the row, and the programme total multiplies the event total by the number of courses as calculated in Table 37. The cell which makes the number of courses calculation was given the name of 'course_num' so that it could be easily referred to from other worksheets in the workbook.

The spreadsheet function used to determine what costs are to be built into each of the columns is the 'If' function. An 'if' statement is a three-part conditional function built into a spreadsheet that allows the user to make an event happen in certain circumstances, and a different event happen if the required circumstances are not met. In the case of this example, the plain English formula for the accommodation cells of each row would be: *If((coding = RH or EA or IA or IN) then accommodation cost = ((day_rate * (duration–1)) + (1*conference rate)), else 0)*.

Study the logic of this formula, for it is key to the whole process of developing the spreadsheet. Once it has been written into the top row accommodation entry, it can be copied down to as many rows as necessary. The named cell values in the formula will always be addressed absolutely to the source value, whereas the cells addressed by their code address will be relative to the row and column that they are in. The coding entry in the formula should therefore be addressed by the code value – eg C6. Table 42 shows that only the codes that meet the criteria in the formula have an accommodation value attached to them. Any other value or blank entry will return a zero value. This approach has been used for the consultant cost, travel cost, video hire cost, equipment hire costs, handout costs, textbook costs and external events costs such as college courses. Each of these can be determined by the use of 'if' statements and linking back to the appropriate named values. One of the advantages of building this sheet in this way is that if the user decides that it is possible to get cheaper accommodation elsewhere, the only cost of accommodation entry that needs to be altered is the one value in Table 38. By this single change the whole workbook, wherever it uses the accommodation value, will update itself, as will any cells using the value in the updated cells. For example, in Table 42 the event total, programme total and cost centre cell would all update themselves at the same time. The worksheet shown here as an illustration deliberately only has a few rows in order to be able to get the example onto one screen. In reality the worksheet would be much bigger, and this rapid updating would be of even greater value.

At this stage it is likely that the budget would be presented to the organisation for authorisation in outline. If the organisation decided that there were modifications to be made, that could be done without necessarily increasing the overall amount spent. Using all of the data that is held in the RDBMS, the development manager can either prioritise the events to cut out those identified as not essential to the achievement of organisational goals or reduce the numbers of people scheduled to attend each programme, again by prioritising based on information gathered at the appraisal which classified needs in relation to the achievement of the job essentials. Undertaking the exercise in this way ensures that any development that falls by the wayside is not crucial to the effectiveness of the organisation in the short term.

Phasing the budget

Let us now suppose that the budget has been agreed at the amount of £69,195. It is not as simple as saying 'That is the money we have to spend for the year, and we can spend it when we like.' The budget spending needs to be phased throughout the year. Even then it will be dependent on the business's achieving the income forecast and keeping other costs to the budget forecast. If these two things do not happen, it is unlikely that the development budget will be released as forecast. However, let us assume that the budget is forthcoming as forecast: when will we need the money?

Table 43 shows a further worksheet modelled on the

Table 43
PHASING THE BUDGET

		JAN	FEB	MAR	APR	MAY	JUN	JUL	AUG	SEP	OCT	NOV	DEC
APPRAISAL	18540	1	1	1									
		6180	6180	6180	0	0	0	0	0	0	0	0	0
ASSERTION	5370				1					1		1	
		0	0	0	1790	0	0	0	0	1790	0	1790	0
FIRST AID	4650			1			1						1
		0	0	1550	0	0	1550	0	0	0	0	0	1550
WORD PRO	9300				1	1	1						
		0	0	0	3100	3100	3100	0	0	0	0	0	0
SPRDSHT	2460	1								1	1		
		820	0	0	0	0	0	0	0	820	820	0	0
RECRTMNT	17220		1				1					1	
		0	5740	0	0	5740	0	0	0	0	0	5740	0
SALES SKILL	6780	1		1				1					
		2260	0	2260	0	0	0	2260	0	0	0	0	0
IPD PROG	4875									3			
		0	0	0	0	0	0	0	0	4875	0	0	0
MONTHLY PHASING		9260	11920	9990	4890	8840	4650	2260	0	7485	820	7530	1550
TOTAL =													
£	69,195												

information contained in the workbook so far. It is a relatively simple matrix of the months of the budget year and a row for each type of development event in the budget. Not visible on this screen but located in a separate part of the workbook, as already explained, are all of the associated values for this screen. From previous screens we can automatically derive the overall cost of each programme of events. Each time an event is to be held, the number is placed in a month cell, and the cost of the event can be made to appear underneath it, as in the January cell for the appraisal programme. In this example the worksheet totals the number of individual events to be held: if it exceeds the budgeted amount, the screen gives a warning that the group of events will be going over budget. This is simple to do by using an 'if' statement which checks whether the (row containing the) number of individual events is greater than the number of budgeted events. If it is it will display the error message: 'This exceeds the budget forecast' at a nominated point on the screen; otherwise it will not display the error message.

The columns for each month total the required spend for that month – information that the finance department will require. There is not much point in taking all of the annual budget out of an interest-earning account at the beginning of the financial year when it may not be required until the tenth month of the year. By adopting this system it will be allocated to the development budget but still be working for the company for as long as possible. There is little technical about this screen except for the 'if' statements checking that the user is within budget: it is an information screen that gives valuable information. It is also crucial to the next section when controlling the budget by variance analysis.

Monitoring the budget by variance analysis

Having defined the size of the budget and the phasing of the budget, the next stage is the implementation of the development plan and actually to spend the money. From all of the information that we have stored within the workbook we can now produce a worksheet that allows us to monitor the monthly forecast against the actual spend, and to produce an

Table 44
CONTROLLING A BUDGET BY VARIANCE ANALYSIS

	JANUARY			FEBRUARY				MARCH			
	FCAST	ACTUAL	VARIANCE	FCAST	ACTUAL	VARIANCE	CUM VARIANCE	FCAST	ACTUAL	VARIANCE	CUM VARIANCE
APPRAISAL	6,180	6,600	(420)	6,180	6,200	(20)	(440)	6,180	5,600	580	140
ASSERTION	0	0	0	0	0	0	0	0	0	0	0
FIRST AID	0	0	0	0	0	0	0	1,550	1,250	300	300
WORD PRO	0	0	0	0	0	0	0	0	0	0	0
SPRDSHT	820	900	(80)	0	900	(900)	(980)	0	0	0	(980)
RECRTMNT	0		0	5,740	5,315	425	425	0	0	0	425
SALES SKILL	2,260	1,900	360	0	0	0	360	2,260	1,800	460	820
IPD PROG	0		0	0		0	0	0		0	0
MONTHLY			(140)			(495)	(635)			1,340	705

instant comparison showing the position with regard to the target.

Table 44 shows a worksheet that achieves this. The sheet is set up by using the figures produced in the monthly phasing worksheet. The corresponding amount for each programme of events appears in the forecast column for each programme. This is not a manual entry: it is a formulated entry produced by referring to the appropriate cell in the phasing worksheet. By entering the data in this way the amount in the phasing cell is automatically entered into the variance analysis. The only cells that require manual entry in the variance worksheet are the figures for the actual amount spent in each category for each month. Indeed, all cells other than actual spend are locked to avoid accidental corruption of the worksheet. The variance is a formulated column which subtracts the actual column from the forecast and reports a positive or negative return.

The example in Table 44 shows three months of the variance analysis worksheet. It can be seen that from month two onwards there is an additional column to show cumulative variance against forecast. These columns simply total the monthly variance columns, again giving a positive or negative value. The final row gives the variance monthly totals. From this screen it is immediately possible for the user to see whether the organisation is over or under budget forecast: the screen follows the accounting convention of showing negative figures in brackets. The example shows that by the end of month three the development budget is £705 under-spent, but in months one and two it was over-spent when appraisal and spreadsheet training went over budget. This information has allowed the development manager to react in month three (March) and recoup the over-spend.

Value for money

The use of financial ratios is a way in which businesses can tell whether or not they are performing well. Among the ratios often used are examples such as profit per employed person and turnover per capita. In a similar way HRM can devise ratios that can give an indication of the effectiveness of its training and development. A common measure for assessing the utilisation of trainers is the number of training days that have been undertaken expressed as total training event days per trainer multiplied by the number of delegates per event. This can give a comparison of utilisation – but not of effectiveness. No one measure alone can satisfy the need to assess a contribution.

In Table 45 a suggested way to assess the relative value for money is to compare the cost per capita of the different forms of training that have been illustrated. Each type of event in the example is associated with a method of training. By simply adding the total training days for each type of event and dividing that into the total cost for the event category, we

Table 45
VALUE FOR MONEY

			NO OF DELS	AVGE DAYS/ EVENT	NO OF EVENTS	TOTAL TRNG DAYS	AVG COST PER TRNG DAY
APPRAISAL	£ 18,540	RH	10	3	3	90	£ 206
ASSERTION	£ 5,370	FA	1	3	3	9	£ 597
FIRST AID	£ 4,650	EX	1	3	3	9	£ 517
WORD PRO	£ 9,300	IC	10	3	3	90	£ 103
SPRDSHT	£ 2,460	IO	6	3	3	54	£ 46
RECRTMNT	£ 17,220	IA	10	3	3	90	£ 191
SALES SKILL	£ 6,780	IN	6	3	3	54	£ 126
IPD PROG	£ 4,875	CO	1	15	3	45	£ 108
	£ 69,195					441	

OVERALL AVERAGE COST PER TRAINING DAY =	£ 157

can arrive at an average cost per training day for each event code. From this we can see that in our examples the most expensive type of event is the external-provider-type course where a delegate needs to stay overnight close to the training event. The best value in terms of cost per training day is the in-house programme undertaken by in-house staff. This measure does not, of course, show the relative effectiveness of the programmes. The course feedback questionnaires should give an indication of that, together with any perceived improvement of performance, as outlined in previous chapters. However, there is a big difference between the two methods in terms of cost – which raises a question that needs to be answered: even if the external provider's programme is effective, does it justify the additional spend or could an alternative be found?

It is true that this illustrative example draws only from a very small sample, but if this worksheet were to be produced summarising all of the programmes run in a full-size training budget, wouldn't such a difference of costs justify scrutiny?

Conclusion

I have shown the processes involved in compiling and managing a training and development budget, and given an illustration as to how a budget application can be set up within a spreadsheet package using the data stored in a HRIS as the source. The spreadsheet package used as an example has been Microsoft Excel 5, but any other modern spreadsheet package would be capable of producing the same output. Although at the beginning of the chapter the spreadsheet was described as a two-dimensional model, that is not strictly the case. Excel 5 and later versions have adopted the convention of being referred to as 'workbooks'. Like any book a workbook consists of pages, or in our vocabulary, worksheets. The power of this feature from the user's point of view is the ability to extract or refer to data from one worksheet and use it in another worksheet. Extraction and/or reference can be a forwards or backwards in the order of the worksheet.

By adopting this method in the examples given, we have been able to minimise the need to input manually from one sheet to another. Yet we have built increasingly sophisticated worksheets as we have progressed, but still by using relatively simple techniques. And, most importantly, we have used the three-dimensional power of the workbook to cause each worksheet to update itself every time a related entry is changed. This feature is powerful – but it can work against the user at times. If you are addressing a cell for information in order to compile another section of the worksheet or workbook, you must want it to be updated in due course with the rest of the workbook. If the information it holds should not be changed, it might be better to enter the value manually or to find a way that locks the cell once the data has been entered.

This chapter has not covered protecting the worksheets: that should be covered extensively in the spreadsheet instruction manual. Nevertheless, a word of warning: it is very easy to corrupt an application that you have spent ages preparing if you do not protect all cells in the worksheet that should not be altered – any cell that will never require manual entry at some time in the future. All spreadsheets afford such protection in various ways. Do not trust to luck. Always keep a back-up copy of the application that is only one session out of date. That way, at least, you will lose only the data from one input session and not the entire application. If the work is saved frequently and an error or corruption occurs, reload from the saved version after first closing the corrupt version *without* saving it.

Finally, with all applications it is a good idea to document the process by writing down what each part of the workbook does and where it gets its data from. The use of cell and range names instead of coded addresses makes debugging so much simpler – which is why this approach is to be recommended.

12

ACTIVE USE OF THE DATA

Throughout this book we have spent a great deal of time discussing developing and building a database and looking at the ways in which it can be used within the business for specific applications. This final chapter looks at how the data that has been stored can be used for wider aspects of application. The reader may feel that the systems specified so far suggest that the applications must be identified in advance. For the most part that is probably true – particularly in respect of the actual data stored. However, once the data has been stored, it can be retrieved and worked with at any time and in any meaningful form. Most organisations know that they will at some time have to review salaries or reward systems. What is not certain is how it might need to be done or what emphasis the organisation may wish to place on any one of its methods of rewarding staff. A RDBMS can assist with this task by making basic data available to be manipulated in whatever way the organisation wishes, even though the analysis may not have been determined before the data was input.

The first examples look at utilising the data to aid in managing pay and benefits. Later examples look at the ways in which the data can be used to evoke organisational indicators regarding trends. In particular, the equal opportunities analysis shows that the data can be retrieved and analysed according to current needs. Certainly, most equal opportunities monitoring will relate to circumstances for which the system is designed, and many basic reports can be predetermined. However, when a specific problem arises it is possible to extract the data and undertake a specific analysis in line with the current need.

Managing pay and benefits

There can be little doubt that one of the major contributions of the HRM function to a business has always been that of managing a pay and reward structure in a way that seeks to give maximum benefits to the organisation, but which enables the organisation to attract and retain the calibre of staff that it requires. There is no point at all in paying too much for staff or, indeed, too little. It is a question of achieving a balance.

The data that has been built up within the suggested RDBMS framework in this book can be manipulated in any way in which the user can perceive a benefit. Because of the relational nature of the way that data has been entered into the system, almost any link that the user might wish to make can be made. Subsequently it is possible for us to undertake an analysis of the data held regarding employee reward in relation to any other parameter that we may wish to. Most organisations seek to pitch their reward package at a particular level in the pay range of the industry or in relation to the location in which they operate. Local chambers of commerce or industry-based associations often carry out and publish a survey that will give employers a guide to the prevailing reward level ranges. How, then, can an organisation check out whether it is getting an appropriate return for its reward package?

The data that is stored can be used to analyse the effects of rewards packages on groups of employees and the effects of changes in such packages. Clearly, one of the best indicators of satisfaction with their employer on the part of employees must be the labour turnover within the organisation. The data stored allows an analysis of the employees' length of service in a very comprehensive manner. The key factors stored are:

- start date with company
- leaving date
- start date in current job
- department
- location
- job type
- grade

- salary
- performance rating
- potential rating.

By linking a query that extracts all of the data fields from the relevant data tables it would be possible to obtain a data set that groups all of the above fields in one table for analysis. If the user wished to be more selective by adding selection criteria, it could easily be done. Possibly only the staff who have joined in the last five years should be selected. Putting a selection criterion into the start date field such as ' > (today–1825)' would cause only records with a date greater than today minus five years to be selected. Similarly, criteria can be entered to limit the selection to set locations or departments, grades or job types. The user decides the criteria: the important point is that the data is there to be excluded rather than not there when the user wants it to be. Indeed, a query can be set up in such a way that the criteria can be altered each time the query is run without the user having to redefine the query. By setting up the query to ask for the criteria for any or all of the data fields, only the specified data will be extracted from the RDBMS.

How should a report be compiled from the data that has been extracted?

The raw data in the query table is not easy for a user to analyse because it is not formatted in the groupings that are required for analysis. A report will have to be set up to do that. In the same way as a query can be formulated to supply the data in different ways or corresponding to different sets of criteria, so too can a report. By setting up a basic report structure and storing it as a report template, the same basic report structure can be reused and modified, which can save a great deal of time. What the system ought to do is group the data and give subtotals of the number of records that fit each grouping. It is not necessary to be able to see every single record: that would be futile, for we have not asked for – and do not need – employee names (for example). Probably the most useful groupings are: by location, by department, by job type

Table 46
STAFF SERVICE ANALYSIS

Location:	Manchester
Department:	Finance
Job Type:	Professional
Grade:	H

Number of current staff	Average Service	Number of leavers in 5 yrs	Average service of leavers	Current average salary	% perform rating of leavers	% perform rating of current	% pot leavers	% pot current
8	24 mths	28	19 mths	£27132	A 10 B 47 C 31 D 11 E 1	A 0 B 12 C 64 D 12 E 12	A 23 B 40 C 35 D 2 E 0	A 12 B 24 C 52 D 12 E 0

and by grade. Within these groupings the individual summaries for each of the other data fields could be shown. Table 46 illustrates what this report might look like for one grouping.

Producing this report shows the strength of the computer. The computer has done what it is best at: sorting, selecting and ordering data. It is not able to draw inferences from the data. Fortunately, this is one skill that human beings do have as well as being able to make external comparisons with factors not stored in the database. The report has supplied the information that we requested, and could provide similar reports for all locations and departments within the organisation. It is now the skills of the human that will further interrogate the report to spot trends and patterns together with the implied messages.

Looking at the report, and assuming that the size of the department has been relatively stable over the five-year period, we can see that the staff at this level in the organisation has turned over three and a half times. The average length of service for leavers has been only 19 months, as opposed to 24 months for those still with the company. Of course, in such a small sample averages can be seriously distorted by one or two anomalies. It is very easy to ask the report to show the maximum and minimum service times together with a standard deviation value as well. This would give a more comprehensive picture. The relative length of service data in isolation does not give a lot of information to work with, but from the salary details it can be seen that the level of manager being analysed at this point is relatively senior within the function. Given the costs of recruiting managers at such a level, a turnover of 350 per cent may be considered too high.

What of the quality of the staff who are leaving compared with the quality of those staying? The details in the report show that a higher proportion of leavers were from the 'A' and 'B' band than the current employees. A similar pattern seems to emerge when comparing the potential of the two groups. This may indicate a problem for the organisation over its ability to retain the more able staff at the level analysed for the department shown. It could equally mean that the staff recruited had aspirations that the company could not in fact meet, and they have therefore chosen to move on. The reason cannot be determined from the information in the report but it does give a basis for further investigation. The profile of the current employees does in fact closely mirror the suggested profile that an organisation might aim for, as outlined in the chapter on appraisals. An organisation is unlikely to be able to cope with too many high-fliers – what it needs is a majority of good-quality employees who are achieving and maintaining the accountabilities they are expected to. The example report shown here indicates that this is what is happening. Without this analysis the organisation could have the feeling that it is losing too many able people and might be tempted to increase the rate of remuneration in order to try to retain them. Yet the report shows that the current employees have a 24-month average length of service and are generally perceived as at least achieving job requirements.

A further interpretation of the report could be that there has been a tendency to recruit people who have been looking for more than the organisation can offer and who are more able than it needs. Instead of changing the remuneration rate, or trying to retain overambitious people, it might be better to develop a more realistic person specification, and recruit to that standard.

It is not possible to define or discuss every possible combination of data fields and report analysis in this book. This simple illustration is meant to act as a catalyst on readers, who will be able to determine the important issues for their own organisations and develop or specify the reports that they require to assist in the management of them.

Pay and performance

Much is currently being written about relating performance to pay. The comparative advantages or disadvantages of such a scheme are manifold. What is clear, irrespective of any individual scheme in use, is that the accuracy of the data needed to control or manage the scheme is of paramount importance. Within the RDBMS that we have looked at and developed throughout this book it is relatively simple to extract the type of data that might be needed in order to manage the process. Depending on the scheme, it may be necessary to set up a table to store team performance in relation to achieving goals. These values could be stored monthly or over whatever period of time the organisation uses to assess performance. If the scheme is based on a percentage of salary for a level of performance, it can easily be set up as a query, and the answer table could be exported to the payroll system for inclusion into the payroll. How could that be achieved?

Let us assume that some form of monthly performance assessment of staff, by work team, is necessary for the scheme. The job involved is assigned to a team, rather than to an individual, so by adding a data field to the job table we can associate a job with a work group very easily indeed. We then need to set up a data table consisting of the details of the various groups – this could be under the department name – and assign them a short easy-to-enter identifier code. Finally a data table which we will call 'rel_pay' should be set up with three data fields per record: 'period_number', team identifier, rating. The period number could be coded to indicate month and year (this is not a date-formatted cell and would therefore not be subject to any possible mix-up when the year 2000 arrives); the team identifier could be a code that is entered by using a list-box, as previously described; and the rating might be a simple Y or N to show achievement or non-achievement of targets. It would be the departmental managers who set the targets, not HRM. The query that is raised would need only to identify each employee who is a member of a team that has achieved its target and supply the employee number to payroll. The payroll system would most likely undertake the calculation stage, adding the agreed amount or percentage to the employee's payment.

An additional benefit to the organisation of undertaking the process in this way is that the historical data will build up over time. It will be possible to identify those teams that are achieving their goals consistently, and those that are not. It will be possible to link the data in the team performance data to individual performance data to see if both sets of data are telling broadly the same story. In a scheme where the payment is made annually, based on performance through the year, the data is already stored, either as described above or on the appraisal details table performance rating if a single measurement is the determining factor. It may be that in the case of an annual review based on 12 monthly performances, the employee needs to achieve a standard ten out of 12 event successes. Having once set up a query and report for this, the annual review could be done through the implementation of one single repeat query. A data file could be exported to payroll, and a mail merge letter could be sent to every employee stating his or her own individual entitlement.

The whole database enables the HRM department to assist in the tightening up of the processes by which a business manages its people. This is not to suggest that it is a mechanism designed to restrict employees. It should rather be viewed as a mechanism to help to assure that both parties – employer and employee – receive fair treatment.

In unrelated systems in which there is no method of drawing a comparative link between performance, potential and any benefits increase, it is not possible to easily ensure that underperforming employees do not receive the same pay award as high-achievers (assuming that that is what is desired, and that a pay increase is available). The HRM processes described in this book will enable an organisation to suitably recognise and reward the right staff.

Exporting data to a spreadsheet for analysis

One of the benefits of the rise in the use of RDBMS technology has been the adoption of common standards in the way that data is stored within databases. Most modern database programs use a common format to store data, involving ASCII code to identify characters and numbers, and separating each data field with a comma. This is known as the comma-delimited data format. That is all the average person needs to know about the technicalities of such files. Simply put, it means that we can export data tables or files from our database and import them into other applications. This is the basis of mail merge, by means of which the appropriate data record fields are extracted from a list (usually addresses) and automatically merged into a word-processed document, thereby creating a number of copies of the same basic letter amended to suit the needs of each individual recipient.

A more significant feature of the export/import facility of a database is the ability to export to a spreadsheet application. The RDBMS contains many data tables all of which can be linked in some way. Suppose that it is salary modelling time in the organisation, and it is necessary to consider a number of different approaches before deciding what offer to make to the staff. This could be done within the RDBMS, but it would take time to set up reports and then to amend them afterwards. One of the major features of spreadsheets is the ability to play 'What if?' By utilising the strengths of both types of application, a user can get the best of both worlds.

The first step would be to decide what data we have stored in the main database that we need to export to the spreadsheet, and in what form we need it?

We need the details of the annual pay of every employee – but we do not need their names, only job type or title. It will also be useful to include the department and the location, together with the job grade. If the annual award is dependent on performance, that could also be included. A database query could be built up to generate a table that would contain all of the data so far identified. The table could then be named and saved, thus being stored permanently. Remember: most query answer tables are volatile – which means that they are erased on exit from the program by the user or the next time a new query is run. It is best to have the table saved in case the user inadvertently corrupts the spreadsheet file – at least the raw data can easily be exported again. If the file is saved to a floppy disk or named with an unused table or file name it will not interfere with any other applications.

Each database has a different method of exporting a table, and this should be followed. After the export procedure, the spreadsheet can be loaded with the data. In the example used above, the data is exported to a spreadsheet as a series of columns.

Once the data has been arranged in this way there are a number of things that the user may wish to do to make the data more presentable. First, the data can be sorted and ordered. It might also make sense to move the job title column between the department and grade columns. Remember to highlight the whole area of the spreadsheet that is to be sorted, because the spreadsheet application does not view the row as a record otherwise. If only one column is highlighted and sorted, it will change but the rest of the sheet will not; the worksheet will thus lose its data integrity thereby rendering the sheet useless. A safe way to overcome this is to name the whole range of the data, ignoring the heading row, using a simple name such as 'data', and then when asked what is to be sorted, to type in the name. This preserves the integrity of the database. Another useful addition at this stage may be to add departmental subtotals. Excel can do this automatically by following the instructions in the subtotal choice of the data menu on the toolbar.

Having ordered the data, you should now start developing some 'What if?' scenarios. Compared with the RDBMS it is much easier to add columns to a spreadsheet and to enter formulae into those columns. In a spreadsheet modelling system such as that being described, it is better to utilise a method that allows the whole spreadsheet to update itself at the stroke of a key. A user, when salary modelling, will probably want to know the effect of a specific percentage increase on each department and overall. By utilising 'if' statements and absolute addressing in a formula, a whole spreadsheet can be altered with one entry change.

Table 47 shows a part of a possible database that could have

Table 47

	A	B	C	D	E	F	G
1	job ttl	location	dept	grade	salary	perf rate	increase
2							x%
3	fitter	London	eng	f	12500	C	
4	fitter	London	eng	f	12800	C	
5	fitter	London	eng	f	12200	B	
6	fitter	London	eng	f	11800	D	

been extracted from a RDBMS. The example demonstrates that by altering the value in cell G2 a new salary value conditional on performance can be created. Suppose that the salary award increase for a year was going to be varied according to performance. Any employee achieving a 'C' rating would receive all of the proposed increase, a 'B' or better rating would receive 120 per cent of the proposed increase, a 'D' rating would receive only 60 per cent of the rating, and an 'E' rating would receive no increase. To set this up we need to enter a conditional formula in column G for each row of the database. There are several ways to achieve this within a spreadsheet. This example utilises multiple 'if' statements. Readers might like to explore the 'Look up' functions within their own spreadsheets for an alternative approach.

The multiple 'if' statement to be entered into cell G3 in plain English would be: *(If cell F3 = C then E3*(1 + $G$2), or (If cell F3 = D then E3*(1 + ($G$2*0.6))), or (If cell F3 = A or B then E3*(1 + ($G$2*1.2))) else E3.* This formula uses relative addressing for all cells except G2. This means that it could be copied down the sheet and give the value for each row, requiring the formula only to be typed in for the first row. By absolutely addressing (shown by preceding the characters with a $ sign) the cell G2, all the copied formulae will link back to this cell to receive the basic increase figure. The cell should either be formatted as a percentage cell or have decimal figures entered into it – eg 0.05 for 5 per cent. To understand the formula it is best to think of it as four separate formulae. The first part *'(If cell F3 = C then E3*(1 + $G$2)'* controls what will happen if an employee has a performance rating of C, which the reader will remember signified an achievement of all objectives for the year. Let us assume that the proposed increase is 5 per cent. Now the formula states that if a person has a C rating he or she will receive the full award – ie the current salary times one plus cell G2 (5 per cent). The second part of the formula, 'or (If cell F3 = D then E3*(1 + ($G$2*0.6)))' is a little more complex. It is effectively saying that if a person has a D rating he or she will get only 60 per cent of the basic increase: in this example that would equate to a 3 per cent increase. The expression '($G$2*0.6)' is the part of the formula that dictates this. The third 'if' statement calculates what an employee with a B or A rating will get: '(If cell F3 = A or B then E3*(1 + ($G$2*1.2)))'. Here there are two aspects to draw the reader's attention to. The expression ' = A or B' means firstly that any value equal to A or B in the cell should be treated the same. The second is the expression '($G$2*1.2)': this means the basic award times 120 per cent, or in the example used, an increase of 6 per cent of salary. The final part of the formula, 'else E3' denotes that any other value entered in a performance rating will get no increase: the current salary in E3 will be entered here. The formula could have included an 'If' statement for a performance value 'E' to achieve this, but this would have been overly complex. Additionally, it is a safeguard in case of any erroneous entries or blanks in the performance column. In such a case no increase will be paid for any value other than those included.

Having set the spreadsheet up in this way, we can now change the value in cell G2 knowing that the values calculated in the spreadsheet will always be distributed in the ratios of 120 per cent, 100 per cent, 60 per cent and 0 per cent of whatever basic award the organisation decides it can afford to pay. For any value that the user wants to try, all that has to be done is for the one value in cell G2 to be changed. Once the sheet is set up in this way it does not matter how many rows there are as long as the formula has been copied down to each row. There could be 1,000 employees: the spreadsheet will cope, assuming it has a large enough memory. To finish off the spreadsheet, the user will probably wish to know the total of the existing salary cost, the cost of the increase, and the total of existing cost plus increase. Traditionally, these totals would appear at the bottom of the columns of values. That would be awkward in this case for we will be at the top of the sheet to alter the value in G2. However, because the spreadsheet does not need to follow this convention, the totals can be put at the top of the sheet by simply adding up the range of cell values for each column total. An even easier way is to name the column range and use the Σ icon button on the toolbar with the named range. By doing this, the totals can be seen as soon as the sheet updates itself when the value in G2 is changed.

There is no need to re-enter the data from the spreadsheet back into the main database. Once the decision has been made regarding the value of the basic increase, the pay data tables can be updated and the individual awards can be calculated by introducing a calculation into the data table based on employee performance. This data could then be sent electronically to payroll and an individual letter could be generated to each employee. The benefit of undertaking the review in this manner is that there is a minimal danger of corrupting the main database while modelling scenarios, and that only the final amendments are made to the database, thereby minimising the amount of work that has to be done within the RDBMS.

There will be many reasons why a user might wish to export data from the database for modelling purposes. This chapter has used one example as a way of illustrating the combined power of the relational database and the spreadsheet. There are other techniques that can be used. A particularly useful summarising tool within Excel 5 is the 'Pivot table', which represents an extremely quick way for the user to summarise data variables, group them in different ways, and present them as totals, counts of occurrences, average values, or minimum or maximum values in specified groupings. As a way of extending knowledge beyond this book, the reader might like to explore the Pivot table option: it can be found in the data menu of the main menu in Excel, and there are instructions in the Help function.

Managing the holiday year

Although this topic was discussed in an earlier chapter, it is worth taking a further look. It may well give the reader some new ideas.

In an organisation in which annual holiday entitlement is taken by the employee at arbitrary times, it is important for the organisation to be able to manage the process. Many organisations have found that as the holiday year comes to a close employees have to cram outstanding holidays in, carry some forward, or lose them. Occasionally, organisations might allow payment in lieu of outstanding holidays, but this can wreak havoc with the cash-flow forecasts of the business. In earlier chapters we talked about the keeping of attendance records which included the logging of holiday dates. This logging could easily be extended by authorising an unused code such as 'PH' to signify a proposed holiday. The entry of this code together with the start and finish date would give valuable planning data. A report can be produced that analyses the amount of the holiday year left, the number of holiday days actually taken, the number of intended holiday days booked, and the number of holiday days unallocated. This report could be produced on a monthly basis for each department, or any other meaningful division in the company. The report would be circulated to line managers, and where there were large amounts of unbooked holidays the manager concerned could be asked to rectify the position.

This process may seem to be something of a 'Big Brother' approach, but it should help prevent anyone's having to try to take over holiday from a previous year. If a holiday could not be fitted in in the previous year, how will it be fitted in the current year together with this year's entitlement? Additionally, holidays are intended to help employees recharge their batteries. The implication is that individual performance may suffer without holidays. It must therefore be in everyone's interest to take holidays at the appropriate time. This simple method of logging intended and actual holiday can enhance the HRM process and the quality of the information that it can provide to the business.

Managing equal opportunities

Although this topic has been talked about at various points within this book, it is worth mentioning it again in this, the final chapter. With the data that is now stored in the system and the historical development of the data, it is possible for an organisation to undertake a regular analysis of its behaviour in all areas that relate to equal opportunity, both from the legal viewpoint and from a moral viewpoint. Clearly, in any report that is analysing an area of the employee database, further groupings could be introduced to take into account of ethnic origin or gender. To do this may have some uses – but it is probably better to set up a series of reports that deliberately show the information that is required rather than collate such data as an add-on to other reports. With the data that is included in the system we can monitor such areas of activity as new starters, promotions, dismissals, leavers, pay awards, comparative salaries, absence, performance ratings, potential ratings, succession identification to new jobs, job grading, allocation to categories of jobs, and development opportunities and activities. Any of these topic areas could be analysed by the system in respect of gender, ethnic origin, age, or whether an employee is skilled/unskilled. Such reports can be produced quarterly in relation to any organisational division that is meaningful – for example, by department or location. If it is suspected that there may be a problem, the reports could even be produced in respect of behaviour by manager or supervisor. Many of the reports would be easier to analyse if they were presented in graphic form, perhaps as pie-charts. A gender comparison of employees in specific jobs can be easily represented in this way as can a comparison of ethnic mix. Given that the government publishes the statistics regarding indigenous ethnic mix each decade, it may be useful to relate ethnic mix reports to the actual indigenous population ratios for the catchment area of the organisation as a fair benchmark of what might be expected of the organisation. It is expected that the overall profile of staff employed should reflect the ethnic mix of the locality.

Conclusion

Chapter 12 has looked at the ways in which the data stored in the RDBMS can be further utilised by the HRM department, and other managers where appropriate, to assist in making decisions about the business based on the best level of information available to them at the time. The last thing that I would advocate is that the vast compilation of all of the data discussed throughout the book should be treated as a passive electronic filing cabinet. The utilisation of the data is limited only by the degree of understanding of what is possible by the system users. The more use that is made of the data in order to assist in making business decisions, the more the organisation will come to expect that the data should help. Individual readers will know what the advantages could be to their own organisations. Where a system exists, this book might help a reader to utilise and adapt it so that it can contribute more. Where a system does not exist but is seen to be needed, it is hoped that this book will help the decision-makers make up their minds about what they require from a system and be able to specify it, rather than settle for what a third party wishes to supply them with.

GLOSSARY

Alpha-numeric character Any alphabetical letter from A to Z, upper or lower case, or a numerical character from 0 to 9. Care should be taken to ensure that a zero is always entered from a number key and not substituted with the letter O. The reverse also applies: a computer will not accept a letter O as a number in a calculation. Some printers distinguish a zero by printing it with a diagonal line in the centre of it. Others show zero as '0' which is narrower than the letter O.

ASCII American Standard Code for Information Interchange. This code ascribes a binary numerical value to letters, numbers and symbols commonly used by computers. By adopting this code, different systems and programs are able to communicate with each other.

Dialogue box An information box that appears on the screen in Microsoft Windows-based software products to inform the user of the next step or to prompt for input from the user.

Expert system An expert system is a software application that makes decisions about what to do next in a particular set of circumstances. Such a system is called an expert system because it is written to cope with a particular function or process. Such systems work best when a decision has to be made quickly but where there are only one or two alternative behaviours.

HRIS Human Resource Information System, usually associated with a computerised system – but an HRIS can also be a paper-based system. Any technique used to store data about employees in an organisation is therefore a HRIS.

Mail merge   The process of merging data fields from a database into a document, often a letter, produced in a word-processing package. The advantage of the process is that the master letter is typed once and the system produces a separate and unique letter for each intended recipient of the letter.

RDBMS   Relational Database Modelling System. Chapter 2 gives a full explanation of a RDBMS. The abbreviated form is used extensively throughout the book.

Volatile table   Information produced by the system that will not be stored permanently in the current format; a data table produced as a result of a particular query request that will be displayed only until a new action is requested. The information can be printed as a permanent record, and it can be renamed with a permanent table name. The query can be re-run at any time to reproduce up-to-the-minute information.

INDEX